MARIANA VANSTIPELEN

TEENAGERS'
WORLD

FACING REAL STRUGGLES, FINDING REAL ANSWERS!

A powerful guide to help teens rise above pressure, pain, and confusion; with purpose and faith.

EDITED AND PUBLISHED BY
SHEKINAH EDITIONS

TEENAGERS'
WORLD TODAY
© 2025 By Shekinah Editions
ISBN: 979-8-89989-075-8 (Paperback)

A publication of the Shekinah Editions.
Scriptures are mainly quoted from the
KJV and NKJV of The Bible.

TABLE OF CONTENTS

PREFACE

Teenagers today are growing up in a world vastly different from the one many of us knew. The pace is faster. The pressure is heavier. The voices speaking into their lives are louder and more confusing. While they are bursting with potential, many are silently battling identity struggles, peer pressure, family conflict, anxiety, and the overwhelming need to simply be accepted.

This book was born out of a deep burden to understand today's teenagers; not just to analyze their behavior, but to truly hear their hearts. Too often, adults either try to control them, criticize them, or completely give up on them. But what teenagers need most is compassion, guidance, truth, and a safe space to grow.

Whether you are a parent, teacher, pastor, mentor, or community leader, you have a unique role in shaping this generation. Our teens are not problems to be solved; they are people to be understood, loved, and empowered. They are searching for identity, purpose, and direction in a noisy world.

We can help them find it, not only by preaching to them, but by walking with them.

This book is a call to action. It goes deep into the real struggles teenagers face: academically, emotionally, financially, socially, and spiritually, and offers practical ways we can respond. More importantly, it reveals how the Church and community can rise up to be the village that every teenager needs.

May this book stir your heart, open your eyes, and inspire you to be part of the solution. Because when we truly see teenagers for who they are and who they can become, we will not only change their story, but we will also change the future for the better.

With love and hope,
Mariana Vanstipelen

A WORD OF THANKS TO GOD

I want to take a moment to give all Glory and Honor to God for the incredible revelation He bestowed upon me. On my birthday this year, 2025, as I sought His guidance and direction for the year ahead, God showed me a vision that would shape the course of this book.

In that revelation, I saw none other than *President Donald Trump* standing before me.

He asked, "What do you do?"

I replied, "I am a pastor, I write books, and I run good works in the world."

Then, he said something that deeply resonated with my spirit: "Listen, can you write a book on the topic of teenagers, their challenges with teachers, money, and more, and how we can help them?"

Without hesitation, I answered, "Alright," and immediately I began to write.

This revelation was a powerful reminder of God's leading in my life and the ways He uses moments to inspire us. It is by His grace that this book has come to life, and I am filled with gratitude for His guidance and wisdom. May He continue to lead and empower all those who read these pages to make a positive impact in the lives of teenagers everywhere.

Glory to God for His revelation, His direction, and His faithfulness.

INTRODUCTION

WHY THIS BOOK MATTERS NOW

We are living in one of the most critical moments in history for teenagers. This is not an exaggeration; it is a reality backed by what we see every day in our communities, schools, churches, and even within our own homes. Depression, anxiety, self-harm, gender confusion, peer pressure, and emotional withdrawal are no longer rare issues; they are alarmingly common.

Teenagers today are navigating a world we could never have imagined when we were their age. They are digital natives, raised with the internet in their pockets and social media at their fingertips. They are constantly exposed to curated images, unrealistic expectations, and the overwhelming pressure to perform, conform, and belong. Their minds are being shaped by endless scrolling, filtered realities, and the loudest voices on the internet, many of which are unwise, unhealthy, and ungodly.

At the same time, our education systems are stretched thin, the homes are often broken or disconnected, and many churches struggle to connect with youth in a meaningful way. Parents feel helpless. Teachers feel overwhelmed. Pastors and youth workers are trying. And teenagers themselves? Many feel misunderstood, unheard, and unseen.

They are asking deep questions:

- "Who am I?"
- "Why don't I feel good enough?"
- "What is my purpose?"
- "Why does no one understand me?"
- "Where do I belong?"
- "Who is actually with me?"

This book was written to answer those cries. It is not just another parenting book or self-help guide. It is a timely resource for *anyone* who cares about teenagers and wants to help them rise above the noise, confusion, and pain of their world. It is a map through the fog. It is a hand extended to both teens and those who love them.

You'll find real issues explored here: the challenges teenagers face with teachers, money, identity, mental health, peer pressure, and even faith. We'll talk honestly about what isn't working; and more importantly, what can. This book does not pretend to have all the answers, but it offers wisdom, tools, and hope drawn from experience, education, and spiritual insight.

Most importantly, this book is also a call to the Church. For too long, the Church has stood on the sidelines, unsure of how to reach the next generation. But the time to wait is over. Teenagers are not the Church of tomorrow; they are part of the Church today. And if we do not rise to disciple, mentor, and walk with them now, we risk losing them to the world.

But there is hope. So much hope.

We have seen what happens when just one adult takes the time to listen, when one congregation creates a safe space, when one school introduces emotional intelligence and life skills, when one youth group prioritizes mentorship, when one community believes in its young people. The change is powerful. It is possible.

This book matters now because teenagers matter now.

They are the next leaders, creators, pastors, inventors, mothers, fathers, and change-makers. If we invest in them today, we will reap a brighter tomorrow. But we cannot help them if we do not first seek to understand them. We cannot guide them if we do not care enough to listen. We cannot heal their wounds if we keep ignoring their pain.

If you picked up this book, it means you care, and that means everything. You are part of the solution. May your heart be stirred, your mind opened, and your spirit empowered to help build a generation of whole, wise, and purpose-driven teenagers.

Let's begin.

PART 1

UNDERSTANDING TODAY'S TEENAGER

Chapter 1

The World of a Teenager Today

1.1 Social Media Pressure

Teenagers today are growing up in a digital world where the boundaries between reality and illusion are blurred. Social media has become their playground, their public diary, their stage, and sometimes, even their battlefield. For many teens, it's hard to imagine life without it. It's where they connect, express, learn, and explore; but it's also where they silently compete, compare, and cry out for validation.

While platforms like Instagram, TikTok, Snapchat, and YouTube offer creativity and connection, they also present a new kind of pressure; one that previous generations never had to face. This is the pressure of *being seen*, *being liked*, *being relevant*, and *being enough* in a fast-moving digital world.

FOMO – The Fear of Missing Out

One of the most powerful forces driving social media pressure among teens is **FOMO**, the *Fear of Missing Out*. Teenagers constantly see snippets of parties they weren't invited to, events they couldn't attend, vacations they can't afford, or relationships that seem perfect online.

Even when they are physically present somewhere, their minds can be far away lost in wondering what they might be missing elsewhere. They scroll, refresh, and tap through stories and reels, not just for entertainment, but out of anxiety that they are being left behind in life.

This creates a culture of *constant comparison*. If someone else seems to be enjoying life more, looking better, gaining more likes, or receiving more attention, then insecurity creeps in. The result is emotional exhaustion, a sense of unworthiness, and the silent question: *"Why isn't my life like that?"*

From a faith perspective, this is deeply spiritual. FOMO can quietly convince teens that they're not enough as they are; when in truth, **God already calls them chosen, loved, and complete in Christ**. Galatians 1:10 reminds us: *"Am I now trying to win the approval of human beings, or of God? Or am I trying to please people? If I were still trying to please people, I would not be a servant of Christ."*

The Illusion of Perfection

Social media rarely shows the whole story. Filters, edits, lighting, and staging all work together to create an illusion of perfection. Teens often forget that most people only post their *highlight reels*, not their struggles or their behind-the-scenes moments.

Yet, when teens scroll through this endless stream of perfect selfies, fit bodies, fun friendships, and luxury lifestyles, they begin to compare it to their *real life*; the pimples, the broken family, the empty fridge, the school stress, the loneliness. The lie slowly forms: *"Something must be wrong with me."*

This emotional and spiritual wound runs deep. It can lead to depression, social withdrawal, anxiety, and low self-esteem. Some teens begin to feel invisible, unworthy, or unloved.

But the Bible speaks truth into this darkness. Psalm 139:14 says: *"I praise You because I am fearfully and wonderfully made; Your works are wonderful, I know that full well."* The pressure to be perfect fades when teenagers begin to understand that they were created with divine intention, not to impress the world, but to glorify God with their lives.

Performing for Likes

For many teens, posting on social media is more than just sharing; it's performing. Every selfie, dance, comment, or joke becomes a way of earning social currency likes, views, followers. But underneath this drive there is a desperate need for *affirmation.*

A post with low engagement might be deleted within minutes. Teens may spend hours taking pictures just to get the "perfect shot." And when they finally hit post, the countdown begins. *How many likes will I get? Who's watching? Did my crush see it?*

The digital applause becomes addictive. The more they get, the more they need. And slowly, without even realizing it, some teenagers begin to tie their worth to the algorithm.

But God does not evaluate us based on filters, fame, or followers. The Lord looks at the heart, not the highlight reel. 1 Samuel 16:7 says: *"People look at the outward appearance, but the Lord looks at the heart."* Teens need to be reminded that their value doesn't come from virtual applause; it comes from being *children of the Most High God.*

Losing Real Connection

Ironically, the more connected teenagers are online, the more disconnected many of them feel in real life. Some teens sit together in a room but speak only through snaps or DMs. Real conversations are replaced with emojis. Laughter is replaced with reaction buttons. And deep friendships are replaced with streaks and follows.

This digital version of community is often shallow. Teens may have hundreds of followers and still feel completely alone.

The Church has a powerful role to play here. We must help teens re-discover *real connection*. Jesus spent time sitting with people, listening, walking with them, eating together, and sharing life. The early Church in Acts 2:42-47 is a beautiful example of fellowship, unity, and authentic relationship.

Teens today need more than likes; they need love. They need adults and mentors who will look them in the eyes, ask how they're doing, and wait for the real answer. They need friends who care about their hearts, not just their posts.

Using Social Media With Purpose

Social media isn't evil. It's a tool, and like any tool, it can be used for good or harm. The goal is not to throw it away, but to use it **wisely, purpose-fully, and with balance**.

Teens need guidance in setting healthy boundaries:

- Limiting screen time
- Turning off notifications during study or sleep
- Taking social media fastings
- Following people who inspire, not drain
- Posting from a place of truth, not insecurity

They also need to be encouraged to use their platforms for good. Instead of craving popularity, what if Christian teens started sharing truth, hope, and faith online? What if they used their influence to lift others up instead of comparing? What if they became digital disciples: *salt and light* even in the virtual world?

Romans 12:2 reminds us: *"And do not be conformed to this world, but be transformed by the renewing of your mind, that you may prove what is that good and acceptable and perfect will of God."* Teens need this renewal daily. Because when their minds are filled with truth, their hearts become stronger, and the pressure of social media loses its grip.

1.2 Identity Struggles

Perhaps one of the deepest and most defining questions a teenager asks silently or out loud is:

"Who am I?"

It's a question of identity, one that shapes how they see themselves, how they interact with others, and how they imagine their future. In today's world, the pressure to answer that question quickly and publicly is intense.

From a young age, teenagers are bombarded with messages about who they should be. Advertisements, influencers, movies, and music define what's "cool," "normal," "beautiful," or "successful." Social media adds another layer, offering endless comparison points: what others look like, what they wear, how they act, who they date, what they believe.

The result? Many teens are stuck in a confusing identity crisis. They struggle to define who they are apart from what the world says they should be. And in trying to fit in, they often lose themselves.

The Mask of Approval

Teenagers are in a stage of life where *belonging* matters deeply. They want to be accepted by their peers, liked by others, and seen as "enough." To achieve this, many put on a mask. They may laugh at jokes they don't find funny, wear clothes they're uncomfortable in, or hide parts of themselves to feel accepted.

This "performance" identity is exhausting. Some teens act differently at school, at home, at Church, and online, wearing multiple masks in different spaces just to survive. But deep down, they're still wondering: *"Would anyone love me if they really knew me?"*

God's Word speaks directly to this pain. In **Jeremiah 1:5**, God says: *"Before I formed you in the womb I knew you, before you were born I set you apart."* This means identity is not something we create; it's something we discover through our relationship with the Creator.

God's love is not performance-based. He doesn't love us because we're perfect, popular, or productive. He loves us because we are His children. When teenagers grasp this truth, the masks can start to fall away.

Labels and Lies

Society is quick to label teens based on their mistakes, background, appearance, or abilities:

- "You're the quiet one."
- "You're not smart enough."
- "You're loud."
- "You're too emotional."
- "You are not like your brother/sister."

These labels become internalized. Over time, they shape how teens see themselves and how they behave. What was once someone else's opinion becomes their own belief. And the enemy, satan, feeds off of this, whispering lies that destroy identity and destiny.

The devil is called *the accuser* for a reason. He works overtime to destroy the identity of young people before they even discover it. Why? Because a teenager who knows their identity in Christ is powerful. That teen will walk in authority, purpose, and confidence.

As believers, we must speak the **truth** louder than the lies. Ephesians 2:10 declares: *"For we are God's masterpiece. He has created us anew in Christ Jesus, so we can do the good things He planned for us long ago."* Every teenager needs to hear this, again and again.

The Pressure to Define Yourself

In today's culture, teenagers are being told that they must define and express who they are and *do it early*. They're asked to label their values, personality, and goals, often before they've even finished growing.

Instead of allowing time for discovery, society rushes teens into *self-definition*. And if their identity doesn't fit into the world's current trends, they may feel rejected or confused. Many are left wondering:

- "Am I enough as I am?"
- "What if I don't know who I am yet?"
- "Why do I feel like I'm the only one struggling?"

But Scripture gives us a healthier path. In Colossians 3:3b, Paul writes: *"... your life is now hidden with Christ in God."* What a powerful image; your true self is hidden in Christ. It's not something you need to invent. It's something you uncover, layer by layer, as you walk with Him.

The Church must become a place where teens can take off the pressure to "have it all figured out." We must remind them: you are on a journey. You're allowed to ask questions, learn, grow, and change. And through it all, God remains the same: Faithful, loving, and patient.

Comparison Affects Identity

Another dangerous enemy of identity is comparison. When teens measure their worth against others; whether it's grades, followers, talent, or looks; they either feel *less than* or *better than* someone else. Both extremes are dangerous.

Comparison robs joy and blinds teenagers to the unique gifts God placed in them. A teen who compares their singing voice to a famous artist may not discover their anointing to lead worship. A girl who compares her body to models may not learn to appreciate the temple God gave her.

God didn't create duplicates; He creates originals. Psalm 139:13 says: *"For You created my inmost being; You knit me together in my mother's womb."* That "knitting" was a deliberate and beautiful process, unique to each person. No one else has the exact combination of talents, characteristics, and potential that you do. When teenagers begin to understand that they are one-of-a-kind masterpieces, they are freed from the suffocating grip of comparison. They can embrace who they are without needing to measure up to anyone else's standards.

The Church's Role in Helping Teens Find Their Identity.

The Church has a crucial role to play in helping teens discover and embrace their true identity in Christ. It must be a safe space where they can wrestle with questions, make mistakes, and experience growth without fear of judgment. The Church should provide guidance, support, and a foundation of truth; pointing them to their Creator as the source of their worth and purpose.

Teens need mentors who will walk alongside them, listening to their struggles, encouraging them in their faith, and reminding them of their identity in Christ. We must help them understand that their worth is not found in their achievements or how they are perceived by others, but in who they are as children of God.

The Church must also offer opportunities for teens to serve, allowing them to see how God is using them to make a difference. Serving others helps teenagers understand that their identity is not defined by what they receive, but by what they give. It also opens their eyes to the needs around them, shifting their focus from self-centeredness to Christ-centeredness.

God's Truth About Identity. Ultimately, the most important truth teenagers need to understand is that their identity is anchored in God. In 1 Peter 2:9, the apostle Peter declares: *"But you are a chosen generation, a royal priesthood, a holy nation, His own special people, that you may proclaim the praises of Him who called you out of darkness into His marvelous light;"* This passage reminds teens that they are chosen, valuable, and set apart for a special purpose.

When teens know who they are in Christ, they can stand firm in their identity, even in the face of adversity or confusion. They can reject the lies of the enemy and embrace the truth of God's Word. They can walk confidently into their future, knowing that they are deeply loved, uniquely created, and called by God for a divine purpose.

As the Church comes alongside them in this journey, we can help shape a generation that is secure in their identity, empowered to fulfill their calling, and determined to live lives that glorify God.

1.3 Cultural and Generational Gaps

One of the most significant challenges in understanding today's teenagers is the growing cultural and generational gap between them and the older generations. The world in which teenagers live is vastly different from the one their parents and teachers grew up in, and this gap can often lead to confusion, frustration, and even conflict. Understanding and navigating this divide requires not only empathy but a deeper acknowledgment of the forces shaping the lives of today's youth.

The Role of Technology in Shaping Teenagers' Lives

The most obvious difference between generations today is the role of technology in shaping daily life. Teenagers are often described as "digital natives"; a generation born into a world where smartphones, social media, and instant access to information are a constant presence. The digital landscape has revolutionized how teenagers communicate, learn, and form relationships. Unlike previous generations, who relied on face-to-face communication, written letters, or phone calls, today's teens are always connected. Social media platforms such as Instagram, Snapchat, TikTok, and YouTube are not just entertainment tools but social spaces where teenagers express their identities, form communities, and make sense of their place in the world.

While this digital world offers many benefits, such as access to vast amounts of information and the ability to form global connections, it also comes with its own set of challenges. The constant exposure to online content, including social media posts, influencers, and viral trends, creates immense pressure for teenagers to conform to certain standards. This can lead to feelings of inadequacy, anxiety, and a distorted sense of reality. For many teens, their online persona may differ drastically from their real-life identity, which complicates their ability to navigate both worlds.

The generational gap here is obvious: Older generations may struggle to understand the complexities of online interactions, the pressure to maintain a "perfect" digital presence, or the constant need for validation that many teenagers experience. This divide can lead to misunderstandings, as adults may see social media as a shallow or superficial aspect of life, while for teens, it's often a critical space for self-expression and connection.

The Changing Landscape of Values and Beliefs

Beyond technology, teenagers today are growing up in a rapidly changing world with a different set of values compared to previous generations. Social justice movements, diversity, and inclusivity have taken center stage in today's cultural discourse.

Teenagers are more aware of social inequalities, whether related to race or economic status, and are often vocal about their desire to create a more inclusive, fair, and equal society.

The rise of movements and environmental activism has had a profound impact on the way teenagers perceive the world and their role in it. They are more likely to question traditional beliefs and challenge societal norms. This can create tension between them and older generations who may hold more conservative or traditional views. For example, debates over issues such as gender equality or climate change can be polarizing, with teenagers pushing for change while older adults hold onto long-standing beliefs.

Furthermore, teenagers today are more likely to reject the idea of a "one-size-fits-all" worldview. They are more individualistic, searching for unique ways to express their identities, be it through fashion, music, or their beliefs. For older generations, who may have grown up with a more uniform or prescribed set of values, this quest for individualism can seem perplexing or even unsettling.

The generational gap here lies in the different ways these values are formed and passed down. Parents and teachers may feel a sense of responsibility to impart their own values and worldview to the next generation. However, this can sometimes come across as dogmatic or restrictive to teenagers, who are looking for autonomy in shaping their identities. The challenge for parents and mentors is to find a balance between guiding teenagers and allowing them the freedom to explore their own values.

The Impact of Cultural Shifts on Family Dynamics

The generational gap isn't limited to external societal pressures; it also deeply affects family dynamics. The structure of the family unit has changed significantly over the years. While previous generations may have grown up with more traditional family roles; father as the breadwinner, mother as the caregiver, today's families are more diverse and fluid in terms of roles and expectations. Single-parent households, blended families, and non-traditional family arrangements are more common, which means that teenagers may be navigating complex home lives that differ from those of their parents or grandparents.

The breakdown of traditional family structures can create additional challenges for teenagers. In some cases, teenagers may be raised in environments where they have to take on adult responsibilities, such as caring for younger siblings or financially contributing to the household. In other cases, strained relationships between parents or caregivers may lead to emotional or psychological stress for the teenager. This dynamic can often cause tension when parents or adults in the teenager's life do not understand the weight of these challenges, viewing them through a lens of traditional family expectations.

Moreover, communication within families has also evolved. Many teenagers today may prefer texting or messaging rather than talking face-to-face, which can lead to misunderstandings or a lack of emotional connection. Parents who grew up with more direct, in-person communication may struggle to connect with their teenagers in a meaningful way. The ability to listen and engage with teenagers in a way that validates their emotions and experiences is essential but often requires a level of understanding and flexibility that older generations may not be accustomed to.

The Influence of Pop Culture and Peer Pressure

Another key factor contributing to the cultural gap is the influence of pop culture and peer pressure. For teenagers, peer validation and acceptance are crucial components of their social identity. The desire to fit in and be accepted by their peers often drives their behavior, influencing their fashion choices, music tastes, and even the way they speak.

Pop culture; through music, film, and social media, plays a huge role in shaping the attitudes, desires, and beliefs of teenagers. This can sometimes create tension with older generations who may have different tastes, values, or experiences with pop culture.

For instance, the rise of influencers and content creators on platforms like YouTube and TikTok has created an entirely new way for teenagers to aspire to success. Unlike previous generations, who may have looked up to athletes, actors, or politicians, today's teenagers are more likely to idolize online personalities who have gained fame through social media. Parents and teachers may find it hard to relate to this new model of success or even understand the level of influence these social media figures have on their children.

The pressure to conform to trends; whether in fashion, behavior or interests, can also create a sense of insecurity in teenagers. For those who are not able to keep up with the latest trends or gain the approval of their peers, feelings of alienation can set in. Adults, who may have been raised in a different cultural context, may not fully grasp the intensity of this pressure, which can lead to frustration on both sides.

Bridging the Gap: The Role of Empathy and Understanding

To effectively bridge the generational and cultural gap, it is essential for both teenagers and adults to engage in open, honest, and empathetic conversations. Parents, teachers, and mentors must take the time to understand the pressures and challenges that teenagers face in today's world, from the influence of technology to the complexities of identity formation. This requires a willingness to listen without judgment, validate their feelings, and recognize the unique circumstances that shape their lives.

At the same time, teenagers must also be willing to listen to the perspectives and wisdom of older generations. While it's important for teens to assert their own identities and challenge societal norms, there is also value in learning from the experiences of parents and mentors, they are valuable sources of support and guidance, and their insights can provide important context for making wise decisions in an increasingly complex world.

Building bridges across generations takes patience and effort, but the reward is a stronger, more empathetic connection that allows both teens and adults to learn from one another and navigate the challenges of today's world together.

Chapter 2

The Teenage Brain

2.1 How Teens Think and Feel

Adolescence is a unique developmental phase marked by rapid brain growth, emotional intensity, and evolving social identity. During this period, teens are navigating the complex journey between childhood dependency and adult independence. This transition is not just behavioral, it is deeply neurological.

The Adolescent Brain: A Work in Progress

Scientific research reveals that the teenage brain is still under construction. While the brain reaches about 90% of its adult size by age six, the structural and functional development continues into the mid-twenties. Two critical areas of the brain shape how teens think and feel: the **prefrontal cortex** and the **limbic system**.

The prefrontal cortex, responsible for decision-making, impulse control, planning, and foreseeing consequences, is among the last regions to fully mature. This means teens often rely more on the limbic system, the emotional center of the brain, to process experiences and make decisions. As a result, emotions can overshadow logic, and risk-taking or impulsive behavior becomes more common.

This neurological imbalance does not mean teens are irrational or immature in all aspects. Rather, their brains are wired to prioritize emotional and social learning during this stage, which is essential for building identity and independence. However, it also makes them more vulnerable to peer pressure, mood swings, and emotional reactivity.

Emotional Intensity and Sensitivity

Teenagers experience emotions more intensely than children or adults. This is partly due to hormonal changes during puberty, but also because of how their brains interpret emotional stimuli. MRI studies show that teens often interpret facial expressions, especially ambiguous ones, more negatively than adults. For example, a neutral look might be seen as a judgmental glare, leading to misunderstandings and conflict.

Additionally, the emotional highs and lows of adolescence can feel overwhelming. Joy, anger, sadness, and excitement are often amplified. A minor disagreement with a friend might feel like a betrayal; a compliment may trigger euphoric self-confidence. These fluctuations are not exaggerated for attention; they reflect genuine neurological and emotional responses.

This is why emotional support, validation, and careful communication are essential when working with teens. They need adults who can remain calm, present, and empathetic even when their own emotions are stormy.

The Quest for Identity and Belonging

Teenagers are on a quest to answer fundamental questions: *Who am I? Where do I fit in? What do I believe?* This search for identity affects how they think about themselves and others. They begin to challenge authority, question previously accepted truths, and explore different roles, styles, and ideologies.

Social belonging becomes a powerful force. Peer approval can influence decisions more than adult advice. Teens may adopt group behaviors, even risky or rebellious ones, not out of defiance, but out of a deep desire to be accepted. This is normal, not pathological. Belonging to a group helps adolescents test boundaries, build confidence, and find their voice.

Yet, the fear of rejection can also heighten anxiety, insecurity, and emotional pain. Teens may appear moody or withdrawn when, in fact, they are navigating a world filled with new social complexities, from school dynamics to online interactions.

Moral and Abstract Thinking

As their cognitive abilities expand, teens begin to think more abstractly. They can reflect on hypothetical situations, understand metaphors, and engage in ethical reasoning. This development allows them to explore values, beliefs, and long-term goals.

However, because their brains are still learning how to integrate emotions and logic, their moral reasoning may be idealistic or inconsistent. A teen may advocate for justice and fairness but act selfishly in a group setting. This apparent contradiction is part of their cognitive growth and should be met with guidance, not condemnation.

Adults should encourage open-ended conversations that help teens think through their beliefs and choices. Ask reflective questions, rather than offering immediate answers. Empower them to own their opinions and to learn from experience.

Risk, Reward, and the Teenage Brain

One of the most distinctive features of teen thinking is an increased sensitivity to rewards. Dopamine, the brain's "pleasure chemical," is especially active in adolescents. This makes new experiences, thrill-seeking, and social approval feel extremely rewarding. It also means teens may undervalue long-term consequences in favor of short-term gratification.

This is why teens might take risks even when they "know better." Knowledge and behavior do not always align, because their developing brains weigh reward more heavily than risk. This is not an excuse for irresponsibility, but a framework for understanding behavior.

Constructive risk-taking, such as sports, creative arts, travel, and public speaking, should be encouraged as healthy outlets. These help teens develop confidence, resilience, and self-regulation in ways that benefit their growth.

Empathy, Passion, and Potential

Despite their struggles, teenagers are deeply empathetic, passionate, and full of potential. They care about justice, truth, and making the world a better place. They long to be heard, understood, and believed in. When given the right support and safe spaces, they flourish.

Adults must resist the temptation to label teens as "difficult" or "rebellious" and instead see them as emerging adults in need of mentoring. Consistent, respectful communication and emotional safety are vital. Teens who feel accepted are more likely to open up, cooperate, and grow in maturity.

Teenagers think and feel differently; not because something is wrong with them, but because their brains are wired for growth, exploration, and transformation. By understanding the neurological and emotional roots of adolescent behavior, we can respond with compassion and wisdom. The more we align our expectations with their developmental stage, the more we can guide them into confident, responsible, and emotionally healthy adults.

2.2 Why They Act Impulsively

One of the most common complaints about teenagers is their impulsive behavior. They often act before they think, make questionable decisions, and sometimes engage in risky activities with little regard for consequences. While this may frustrate parents and educators, neuroscience provides a clear explanation: impulsiveness during adolescence is a natural and predictable part of brain development.

The Prefrontal Cortex: The Control Center Still Under Construction

At the center of this issue lies the *prefrontal cortex*, the brain region responsible for decision-making, planning, impulse control, and judgment. This area is sometimes referred to as the brain's CEO because it governs higher-order thinking skills that help regulate emotions and behavior.

In teenagers, however, the prefrontal cortex is still maturing and won't fully develop until the mid-20s. Because of this, teens do not always process consequences logically or inhibit their actions effectively. Instead, they often rely on other parts of the brain, particularly the amygdala and limbic system, which are more emotionally reactive and less rational.

This neurological reality means that when a teen sees a challenge, hears a dare, or experiences strong emotions, their brain is more likely to respond in the moment rather than pause to consider future outcomes. The mechanism that says "stop and think" is not fully online yet.

Dopamine, Reward, and Risk

Another critical factor in teenage impulsivity is *dopamine*, the brain's chemical associated with reward, pleasure, and motivation. During adolescence, the brain's reward system becomes hypersensitive to dopamine. This means that the thrill of doing something new, daring, or socially rewarding produces a powerful emotional response, often more intense than what an adult would feel in the same situation.

This dopamine surge not only motivates teens to seek out exciting or novel experiences, but it also reduces their sensitivity to potential risks. The pleasure center of the brain becomes louder than the warning signs. That's why a teen might speed on a bike, or post something risky on social media, because the rush of reward outweighs the fear of consequences in that moment.

Importantly, this is not a character flaw or rebellion. It's a biological process meant to push young people toward learning, exploration, and independence. However, without guidance and boundaries, it can lead to dangerous behaviors.

Peer Influence and Social Urgency

Impulsivity is often amplified when teenagers are around their peers. Studies show that adolescents are more likely to take risks in the presence of friends than when they are alone. This is not merely social pressure; it's neurological.

When teens are with their peers, the brain's reward centers become even more active. The presence of friends intensifies the emotional reward of an impulsive action. For example, a teen might know that jumping from a high wall is risky, but when others are watching or cheering, their brain may override caution and act to gain approval or admiration.

This tendency reflects a developmental priority: during adolescence, *social belonging* is critical. Teens want to fit in, be accepted, and prove themselves. This drive can lead them to take impulsive risks that they wouldn't consider in a quiet, rational moment.

Emotions Over Logic

Teenagers are also more emotionally driven than adults. Because their *amygdala*; the part of the brain that processes fear, pleasure, and emotional memory is more active than their underdeveloped prefrontal cortex, teens are more prone to "emotional hijacking." This occurs when emotions override logic, resulting in decisions that are fast, reactive, and unfiltered.

For example, a teen who feels insulted may immediately lash out in anger verbally or physically, without pausing to assess the situation. Similarly, a teen feeling rejected might impulsively isolate themselves, post something online they later regret, or make dramatic decisions fueled by emotion rather than reason.

This emotional dominance doesn't mean teens lack intelligence or moral awareness. Rather, it reflects a temporary developmental imbalance where emotions are in the driver's seat more often than logic.

Sleep Deprivation and Its Impact on Control

Many teenagers also experience *sleep deprivation*. which further impairs impulse control. Adolescents need about 8 to 10 hours of sleep each night, yet most get far less due to early school times, homework, digital distractions, and changing biological rhythms.

Lack of sleep significantly affects the prefrontal cortex, reducing its ability to regulate behavior and process information. A sleep-deprived teenager is more likely to be irritable, emotionally reactive, and impulsive. This is not simply about attitude; it's neurological fatigue that impacts how the brain functions.

Supporting healthy sleep habits can improve a teen's emotional stability and decision-making ability, but it requires consistent encouragement, structure, and sometimes advocacy for more teen-friendly schedules in school or activities.

Learning Through Experience

One of the ways the brain learns is through *experience*. For teens, impulsive decisions can also be instructive. They are figuring out what works, what doesn't, and what their limits are. Every mistake offers a lesson.

This is why overly strict control or punishment can backfire. Teens do need boundaries and accountability, but they also need room to grow, experiment, and recover from poor choices. The goal is not to eliminate all risks, but to equip them with tools to think critically, reflect, and take responsibility.

When adults step in with empathy and coaching rather than harsh judgment, teens are more likely to learn from their mistakes and develop stronger internal controls over time.

Strategies for Supporting Impulsive Teens

Understanding why teens act impulsively allows caregivers and mentors to respond with wisdom and grace. Here are a few practical strategies:

1. *Set Clear Boundaries:* Teens need structure. Clearly defined expectations and consequences provide external controls while their internal controls are developing.

2. *Teach Emotional Regulation:* Help teens name their feelings and develop coping strategies like deep breathing, journaling, or talking through decisions before acting.

3. *Model Reflective Behavior:* Demonstrate how to pause, think, and weigh consequences in your own life. Teens learn more by example than by instruction.

4. *Encourage Healthy Risks:* Channel their desire for novelty into positive outlets: sports, arts, volunteering, leadership roles, where they can experience thrill in safe environments.

5. *Stay Connected:* Maintain open communication. Teens are more likely to listen and reflect when they feel supported, not judged.

6. *Celebrate Growth:* Acknowledge progress in self-control and maturity, even in small steps. Positive reinforcement strengthens future wise decision-making.

Teenage impulsiveness is the natural outworking of a developing brain. While it can lead to frustrating or even dangerous moments, it is also part of how teens learn, grow, and mature. When adults understand the biological and emotional reasons behind impulsive behavior, they can guide teens with patience, wisdom, and compassion.

By creating safe spaces, offering consistent guidance, and modeling thoughtful behaviors, we can help teenagers navigate their impulses and gradually develop the wisdom they need for adult life.

2.3 The Science Behind Their Decisions

Have you ever looked back at a decision you made and wondered, "What was I thinking?" Maybe you texted someone something you wish you hadn't, said yes when you should've said no, or took a risk that didn't end well. If so, you're not alone, and more importantly, you're not broken. There's actually a *real science* behind why teenagers often make quick, risky, or emotionally driven decisions. Understanding it doesn't just help you avoid future mistakes; it empowers you to make stronger, wiser choices.

Your Brain is Still Growing, and That's a Good Thing

Let's start with the basics: your brain is still under construction. That might sound strange, but it's true. The human brain doesn't fully mature until your mid-20s. One of the last parts to finish developing is the prefrontal cortex, which is the area just behind your forehead. This region is responsible for things like:

- Thinking ahead

- Controlling impulses

- Making long-term plans

- Weighing consequences

- Solving problems logically

In other words, it's the part of the brain that helps you pause and think before doing something. Since it's still maturing in your teenage years, sometimes your brain doesn't fully connect actions with their possible outcomes right away. That's not because you're not smart. In fact, teenagers are incredibly sharp and capable of deep thought. But your brain is still *training* to work like a wise adult's brain.

The Role of the Limbic System

While your prefrontal cortex is still growing, another part of your brain called the **limbic system** is already fully active, and very powerful. This area handles your emotions, rewards, and motivations. It reacts quickly, especially to things like:

- What feels good

- What feels exciting

- What feels unfair

- What brings approval from others

This is why sometimes you feel like your emotions are running the show. In many cases, they are. Your brain is wired during these years to be emotionally intense and *sensitive to rewards*. That's part of what helps you grow into your identity and develop strong passions. But it also means your brain sometimes pushes you to act fast, before logic catches up.

Why You Crave New Experiences

Teen brains are wired to explore. Your brain releases a chemical called dopamine, especially when you try something new or exciting. Dopamine gives you that "yes!" feeling when you take a risk and it pays off. This is why teens often seek out new experiences, even if they're a little dangerous.

Trying new things isn't bad; it's actually how you grow, learn, and become independent. But without a fully developed decision-making center, your brain might focus more on the thrill than the risk. That's why teens are statistically more likely to:

- Try risky stunts

- Experiment with substances

- Make quick social media posts

- Say something they could later change

It's not because teens don't care; it's because their brains are experiencing reward signals more strongly than adults This isn't a flaw. It's part of how your brain is teaching you what excites you, what you enjoy, and how to take control of your own life. The key is learning how to balance that excitement with smart thinking.

The Influence of Friends

Have you noticed how much more confident or daring you feel when your friends are watching? There's a reason for that. Science shows that teens are more likely to take risks when they're around peers. Your brain is wired to care deeply about what others of your age think of you.

This isn't a weakness; wanting to be liked and accepted is a natural part of growing up. But it can affect your decision-making. For example:

- You might join in on something risky just to avoid feeling left out.

- You might post something online for likes even if it goes against your values.

- You might stay silent when you should speak up, just to avoid judgment.

Learning how to think for yourself while still staying connected to your friends is one of the most important skills you'll ever build. That takes time and courage.

So, What Can You Do About It?

Now that you know your brain is still developing, you might wonder, "Does that mean I can't make good decisions?" Absolutely not. In fact, the more you *understand your brain,* the stronger your decision-making can become. Here are some practical tips that work with the science of how your brain grows:

1. Pause Before You Act

Even a 5-second pause before reacting can help your brain switch gears. When you feel emotional, challenged, or tempted, take a breath. Ask yourself:

- "If I do this, what could happen next?"

- "Would I still do this if no one was watching?"

- "Will I feel good about this tomorrow?"

These simple questions help activate your prefrontal cortex, giving you a chance to think before you leap.

2. Think Long-Term (Even Just a Little)

Your future might feel far away, but your decisions today shape it. That doesn't mean you have to stress about everything, but try imagining:

- "How will this affect me in a week?"

- "Will this build or break trust with someone I care about?"

- "Am I choosing what's easy, or what's wise?"

Even short-term vision can help build long-term maturity.

3. Find Safe Ways to Take Risks

You're wired to seek adventure, so choose your challenges wisely. Look for *healthy risks* that let you grow and discover yourself:

- Join a new club or try a new sport

- Start a creative project

- Speak in public

- Volunteer in a new setting

These kinds of experiences satisfy your brain's desire for something new while building your confidence and character.

4. Surround Yourself with People Who Think Bigger

Not all influences are equal. Your brain picks up on the mindset of the people around you. Try to build friendships with those who:

- Respect themselves and others

- Have goals and values

- Can say no to peer pressure

- Encourage your growth

That doesn't mean avoiding everyone who's struggling, just choose your inner circle with intention.

5. Learn

It's part of how we grow. Instead of hiding your mistakes or beating yourself up, reflect on them:

- What led me to that choice?

- What can I do differently next time?

- Who can help me grow in this area?

Mistakes are painful, but they are also powerful teachers; especially when you're willing to learn and move forward.

You're in Training

The next time you make a decision that surprises you; good or bad, remember this: your brain is in training. You're not behind, broken, or immature. You're developing the very skills that will make you wise, independent, and strong. You'll surely face many moments of breakthrough, growth, and victory.

The science behind your decisions isn't meant to excuse bad choices. It's meant to help you understand yourself better, so you can own your decisions with courage and wisdom.

You have what it takes to make powerful, life-shaping choices. And now you know: your brain is on your side. It just needs time and your partnership to become the strong, sharp, and thoughtful tool God designed it to be.

Chapter 3

Who Influences Teenagers?

3.1 Parents, Peers, pop culture

As a teenager, you're constantly growing, learning, and shaping your identity. One of the biggest questions during this stage of life is: *Who is shaping you?* Whether you realize it or not, your thoughts, choices, and dreams are being influenced every day by three powerful forces: your parents or guardians, your peers, and the culture around you. Understanding how each of these shapes your life will help you decide what kind of person you want to become.

1. Parents and Guardians: The Foundation of Influence

Even if it doesn't always feel like it, your parents or the adults who raise you have a deep and lasting impact on your life. They are the first people who taught you how to walk, talk, relate to others, and respond to the world. As you get older and start becoming more independent, their influence might feel like it's fading, but it's still there.

Parents influence you through:

- *The example they set:* How they handle stress, faith, relationships, and conflict.

- *The values they teach:* Honesty, respect, responsibility, kindness.

- *Their words:* Encouragement, correction, or even silence can leave lasting marks.

Even when teens rebel or pull away, studies show that many teens still care deeply about their parents' approval and often return to their parents' beliefs later in life. If your parents are loving and wise, that's a gift. If they struggle or make mistakes, know that their influence doesn't have to define you. You get to choose what you keep and what you release.

Your takeaway: Parents help shape your foundation. Whether good or bad, their influence matters, but it's not the final word on your future.

2. Peers: The Power of Friends

Your friends are the people you spend the most time with. During your teenage years, they often become your second family. Friends can lift you up or pull you down. That's because peers have an incredible ability to shape:

- How you dress and talk

- What you care about or ignore

- What you laugh at or take seriously

- Whether you feel included or invisible

- The risks you take or avoid

Why do peers have so much power? Because humans are wired for connection and belonging, especially during the teen years. You want to be accepted. You want to be seen. You want to fit in. And there's nothing wrong with that, unless it causes you to abandon your values or go against your better judgment.

The good news is, just like negative peers can pull you down, positive peers can build you up. Friends who share your values, cheer for your goals, and support you through hard times are worth more than gold. You don't need a thousand friends, just a few real ones.

Your takeaway: You become like the people you spend the most time with. Choose friends who respect your identity, not pressure you to change it.

3. Pop Culture: The Voice of the World

Pop culture includes everything from music, movies, and social media, to fashion, celebrities, and trending opinions. Today's teens are surrounded by more content than any generation before; and much of it is designed to grab your attention and influence your choices.

Pop culture can shape how you:

- View relationships and sexuality

- Define beauty or success

- Handle emotions and challenges

- See your identity and future

- Value (or ignore) faith and morality

It often sends the message: *"Be yourself, but only if it looks like this."* It creates trends and pressures that are constantly changing. One day, something is cool. The next day, it's outdated. And in the middle of it all, many teens are left wondering: *"Who am I really, and am I enough?"*

That's why it's so important to guard your heart and mind. Not everything popular is healthy. Not everything trending is true. You have the right to think deeply, question what you consume, and decide for yourself what's worth following.

Remember: culture will try to define you, but only God can give you your true identity.

Your takeaway: Pop culture is loud, but it doesn't have to control you. Be wise about what you let into your heart and mind.

So, Who's Really Leading You?

At the end of the day, you are being influenced, but you also have influence. You can't control everything you're exposed to, but you *can choose what you accept and what you reject.* You're not just a follower of culture, friends, or even parents; you're a leader of your own life.

Ask yourself:

- Who has the most influence on me right now?

- What values do I see shaping my decisions?

- Am I becoming who I want to be or who others expect me to be?

God created you with a purpose. You're not here to copy someone else's path. You're here to walk in your own calling. Surround yourself with voices that lift you higher, and let God's truth be the loudest voice in your life.

You're not just influenced. You're also an influencer. Choose wisely.

3.2 Teachers, Mentors, and Online Voices:

Guiding and Shaping Your Growth

In addition to parents, friends, and pop culture, there are other pow-erful influences shaping the way you think, learn, and grow. Some of these people you meet face to face like teachers and mentors. Others you may not meet, but they still speak into your life through videos, posts, podcasts, or blogs; these are the online voices. Whether you realize it or not, these influences can impact how you view yourself, how you make decisions, and how you see the world.

Teachers: More Than Just School Lessons

Teachers play a key role in your development; not just academically, but emotionally and socially. A good teacher doesn't just explain math or science; they *encourage you to think, ask questions, and believe in your ability to succeed.* They often spend more time with you during the day than even your family, especially on school days

Some teachers challenge you to grow. Others may frustrate you. But each one has the power to influence how you:

- View learning and personal growth

- Handle success

- Communicate with authority figures

- Set goals for your future

The best teachers are not just instructors, but role models. They don't just give you facts; they help you develop character, responsibility, and confidence.

Your takeaway: A teacher's belief in you can open doors in your mind and future. Be open to learning not just subjects, but life lessons.

Mentors: Personal Guides for the Journey

A mentor is someone a little older or wiser who walks with you through life. They may be a coach, youth leader, pastor, or someone else who takes time to know you, listen to you, and help you grow.

Mentors offer something special: *real-life experience and personal guidance.* They've been through things. A mentor doesn't give you all the answers, but they ask you the right questions and help you find the path that's right for you.

Mentors can:

- Help you see your strengths and gifts

- Support you through doubt

- Keep you grounded when you're overwhelmed

- Encourage your dreams and help you stay focused

If you don't have a mentor, pray for one or seek someone you admire. Sometimes, just asking, "Can I learn from you?" can open up a life-changing relationship.

Your takeaway: Mentors help you grow into the best version of yourself. Don't be afraid to reach out and let someone guide you.

Online Voices: Shaping You From a Distance

Whether you're scrolling on TikTok, watching YouTube, or following your favorite influencers on Instagram, the internet is full of people sharing their ideas, opinions, and lifestyles. Some of them are helpful. Some are entertaining. Others may be confusing or even harmful.

Online voices influence how you:

- Think about relationships, success, money, or fame

- View yourself and your identity

- Feel about your faith, your body, and your future

- Compare your life with others' highlight reels

The challenge with online voices is that *you don't always know what's true*. Someone might sound confident or cool, but that doesn't mean they're wise. Some influencers care about your well-being. Others just want clicks, likes, or money.

Always ask:

- Is this person helping me grow or making me feel worse?

- Are they telling the truth or just trying to impress me?

- Does this voice line up with what I believe is right?

Remember, you become like the voices you listen to the most. So choose wisely. Follow people who *build you up*.

Your takeaway: Online voices are powerful. Let truth, wisdom, and Godly values guide who you follow and what you believe.

Who's Helping You Grow?

All around you; teachers in classrooms, mentors in your community, voices online, people are planting seeds in your mind. Some seeds grow into confidence and purpose. Others can grow into fear, doubt, or distraction.

You are not just a sponge absorbing everything; you are *a garden*. You get to decide what you let grow and what you pull out. Stay alert. Stay wise. And surround yourself with people, both near and far, who help you flourish in the person God created you to be.

3.3 The Word of God and the Church:

Anchors in a Shifting World

As a teenager, you're being shaped by many voices: parents, friends, culture, and online content. But above all these, there is one voice that stands above every other: *God's voice through His Word and His Church.* When life feels confusing, when you're unsure who to listen to, or when your heart feels overwhelmed, **the Bible and the Church are safe, steady places to turn to**.

Let's explore how God's Word and His people influence your life, and why they matter more than ever during your teenage years.

The Word of God: Truth That Never Changes

Trends come and go. Opinions shift. What's considered "right" today might be mocked tomorrow. But **the Word of God is the unchanging truth.** It's not just an ancient book; it's a living, breathing message from your Creator. It shows you Who God is, who you are, and how to walk in your purpose.

Here's how God's Word influences your life:

- *It gives you identity:* In a world full of labels, the Bible tells you who you truly are: fearfully and wonderfully made, loved by God, chosen for His purpose.

- *It teaches you how to live:* The Word gives wisdom for real-life situations, friendships, purity, honesty, forgiveness, and how to make good decisions.

- *It strengthens your faith:* When you read the Bible, your confidence in God grows. You begin to see life through His eyes, not just your emotions.

- *It speaks directly to you:* God can use a verse to answer your prayers, calm your anxiety, or give you direction, right when you need it most.

You don't need to be a Bible scholar to start. Just open the Word, ask God to speak to you, and read with an open heart. The more time you spend in the Bible, the more you'll hear God's voice and recognize what's true.

Your takeaway: God's Word is your compass. In a noisy world, it helps you walk in truth, peace, and strength.

The Church: Your Spiritual Family

Some people think the Church is just a building or a weekly service. But the Church is much more; it's *a family, a support system, and a place to grow in your relationship with God.*

As a teenager, you may feel like the Church isn't for you, or like you're too young to be involved. But nothing could be further from the truth. God is calling this generation to rise up and be part of His work, and the Church is the place where you can start living that out.

The Church influences you by:

- *Surrounding you with Godly mentors:* Youth leaders, pastors, and older Christians who care about you and want to help you grow.

- *Providing community:* A place where you can belong, ask questions, share your story, and find friends who share your faith.

- *Offering opportunities to serve:* You can make a difference through music, tech, teaching, evangelism, or helping others.

- *Helping you grow spiritually:* Through Bible teaching, worship, prayer, and fellowship, you get stronger in your faith.

Keep your eyes on Jesus and stay connected to the body of Christ. That's how your faith stays alive and strong.

Your takeaway: The Church is your spiritual home. Don't just attend; belong, grow, and let God use you right where you are.

What Happens When You Stay Connected

When you regularly read the Bible and stay involved in the Church, something powerful happens: your heart becomes strong, your mind becomes clear, and your life becomes fruitful. You learn to live with purpose, resist pressure, and walk in joy.

God's Word and the Church don't just help you survive; they help you *thrive*. They help you discover your calling, overcome temptations, and become the light God has called you to be in your school, your home, and your generation.

Make Space for What Matters

Ask yourself:

Do I spend more time listening to culture than to God's Word?

Do I take time to hear what God says about me?

Am I connected to a Church family that helps me grow?

The Word of God and the Church aren't just for adults. They're for you, right now. *God is speaking to you. The question is: will you listen?*

Stay rooted. Stay connected. Stay in God's presence. When everything else fades, His Word and His people will still be standing.

PART 2

KEY CHALLENGES TEENAGERS FACE

Chapter 4

Challenges with Teachers and the Education System

4.1 Lack of understanding or connection

In today's fast-changing world, one of the most overlooked struggles teenagers face is the lack of understanding or meaningful connection with their teachers. For many young people, school should be a safe and encouraging environment where they are not only educated academically but also mentored, inspired, and understood as individuals. In many cases, this is not the reality.

A Widening Gap Between Generations

One of the main reasons for the lack of connection is the generational gap. Teachers often come from a different world than the one teenagers live in. They were raised in a time without smartphones, social media, or the constant pressure of online comparison. Teenagers, on the other hand, are digital natives. They grow up with a constant stream of information, entertainment, and communication at their fingertips. This difference can lead to misunderstanding, miscommunication, and even conflict.

Many teachers, though well-meaning, may not fully grasp the mental and emotional toll that modern teenage life brings. They may interpret a student's silence as laziness, their distraction as disobedience, or their questions as disrespect. Meanwhile, teenagers may interpret a teacher's correction as personal rejection, their structure as control, or their feedback as criticism rather than help.

When these misunderstandings build up, they form a barrier. Teenagers begin to feel unheard, unseen, and unsupported. This emotional disconnection can lead to a decline in motivation, attendance, and performance. In worse cases, it leads to rebellion, or mental health challenges.

Lack of Emotional Support in the Classroom

Today's teenagers are not just looking for facts and formulas; they are searching for meaning, identity, and someone who genuinely cares. Yet many educational systems prioritize performance. Teachers are pressured to meet academic targets, prepare students for standardized tests, and keep up with administrative tasks. As a result, the emotional well-being of students is often sidelined.

While some teachers do go the extra mile to connect with their students, many are simply overwhelmed. They may lack the training or time to notice the quiet teenager sitting at the back of the class struggling with depression, anxiety, or family problems. And so, teenagers are left feeling alone in a system that is to serve them.

A connected teacher can be a lifeline. Studies show that just one supportive adult in a teenager's life can make a difference. When teachers take time to listen, encourage, and affirm, it builds trust. That trust opens the door for influence; not just academically, but personally and morally.

Cultural and Language Barriers

In multicultural societies, teenagers from migrant or minority backgrounds face an additional challenge; being misunderstood due to cultural or language differences. A teacher may not recognize the struggles a student faces at home, the pressure of translating for their parents, or the internal conflict between two worlds. Misinterpretations can easily arise.

For example, a student who is shy to speak up in class may not be uninterested, they may be afraid of making mistakes in a second language. Or a student who refuses to take part in certain activities may not be rebellious, they may be following religious or cultural practices. Without proper understanding, such students are often misjudged or marginalized.

The Need for Relational Training

If we want to see teenagers flourish in the education system, teachers need to become mentors, not just instructors. Academic knowledge is vital, but so is emotional intelligence. Teachers need to learn how to relate to teenagers with empathy, patience, and discernment. This includes listening more than lecturing, observing behavior with compassion, and creating a classroom culture where questions are welcomed, and differences are respected.

Churches and Christian foundations can also help bridge the gap by offering after-school mentorship programs, teacher-student dialogue events, or emotional intelligence workshops in schools. These programs help teachers understand the realities teenagers face, and help students see their teachers not as enemies, but as potential allies.

A Call to the Church

For Christian communities, this challenge also presents a great opportunity. The Church is uniquely positioned to bring healing into the education system. Teenagers need spiritual fathers and mothers who can model the love of Christ in practical ways. Pastors, youth leaders, and Christian educators can show a different way; a way of care, encouragement, and connection.

Jesus Christ was called Teacher by His disciples, but He was more than that. He ate with them, walked with them, and answered their questions with patience and depth. He connected with them heart-to-heart. That is the kind of teacher teenagers need today.

In conclusion, the lack of understanding and connection between teachers and teenagers is a silent crisis in education. It is not just about poor communication; it is about a missing link. When students feel known, they open up. When they are understood, they begin to thrive. And when they are truly connected to someone who believes in them, they rise to the challenge, not just in school, but in life.

4.2 School Pressure and Academic Stress

School is meant to be a place of learning, discovery, and growth. But for many teenagers today, it has become a major source of stress and anxiety. Instead of nurturing curiosity and a love for knowledge, the academic environment can often feel like a battlefield, where performance, grades, and competition are the only things that matter. Teenagers are under increasing pressure to succeed, to meet high expectations from teachers, parents, and even themselves, and this burden can have a serious impact on their mental, emotional, and spiritual well-being.

The Weight of Expectations

One of the main reasons for academic stress is the overwhelming expectation placed on teenagers to perform. Parents want their children to do well, often hoping they will become doctors, engineers, or lawyers. Teachers, under pressure to deliver good school results, push students hard. Schools, focused on rankings and success rates, create an environment that constantly demands more.

Overloaded Schedules

Today's teenagers have very little free time. Between school hours, homework, extra tutoring, exams, projects, and sometimes part-time jobs, many teens live in a constant state of busyness. Add extracurricular activities like sports, music, or youth group, and the week becomes packed from morning till night.

Even weekends are no longer restful. Assignments are due on Mondays, and many teenagers are attending lessons even on Saturdays. Sleep becomes a luxury. Lack of proper rest leads to tiredness, irritability, and poor concentration. This cycle wears them down physically and mentally.

The Role of Technology and Distractions

While technology can be a helpful tool for education, it has also become a major source of distraction. With constant notifications, social media, and online games, teenagers are often torn between study time and screen time. Many try to multitask; studying with one eye and scrolling through Instagram with the other, but this results in lower productivity and even more stress as deadlines pile up.

Additionally, the digital world creates unrealistic comparisons. A teen may see others posting about high grades, scholarships, or studying in top universities, and begin to feel inadequate. The pressure to "keep up" adds another layer to the already heavy burden of schoolwork.

Exams, Rankings.

Examinations are one of the greatest sources of school-related stress. The focus on passing exams and achieving high rankings often overshadows the process of true learning. In some systems, a student's entire future may depend on a single exam, increasing anxiety and fear.

Students are sometimes ranked publicly, creating competition not just between schools but between classmates. Instead of encouraging one another, teens may feel the need to hide their notes, outperform their friends, or sabotage others to get ahead. This damages friendships and creates a toxic environment of jealousy, comparison, and loneliness.

Mental Health and Emotional Struggles

Academic stress is not just about grades; it affects the heart and mind. Teenagers under constant pressure may suffer from low self-esteem, eating disorders, panic attacks, or suicidal thoughts. Some begin to withdraw from others, stop communicating, or turn to unhealthy coping habits like substance abuse or self-harm.

It's important to recognize that stress doesn't look the same for everyone. Some teens may hide their struggles behind a smile, pretending everything is fine. Parents and teachers must be alert, kind, and willing to listen, not just to correct, but to support.

What Can Be Done?

Creating a Healthy Perspective

Teenagers need to understand that their identity and value are not based on their academic results. They are loved and accepted for who they are, not just for what they achieve. Parents and teachers must speak life, not pressure. Encouraging words, patience, and love go a long way in building confidence.

Balancing School and Life

While education is important, so is rest, family time, spiritual growth, and fun. Encourage teens to take breaks, sleep well, and do things they enjoy. Time with God, reading the Bible, praying, and being part of a youth fellowship can refresh their soul and help them face school challenges with strength and peace.

Encouraging Effort, Not Just Results

Instead of only praising top scores, we should recognize hard work, persistence, and improvement. Not every student will be number one, but every student can grow. God created each young person with different gifts and purposes; some for teaching, others for business, music, or service. Help teenagers discover who they are in Christ.

Seeking Help When Needed

If a teenager is showing signs of stress or emotional struggle, don't ignore it. Encourage them to talk to a school counselor, youth leader, or pastor. The Church should be a safe place where young people can open their hearts and receive prayer, support, and healing.

School pressure is real, but it does not have to crush the next generation. With the right balance of love, discipline, support, and prayer, we can help teenagers face academic stress with courage, wisdom, and hope. As they learn to trust God, discover their identity in Christ, and grow in character, they will find strength to overcome every challenge, and thrive.

4.3 Discipline, bullying, and school rules

Teenagers spend a significant portion of their lives at school. It is a place where they not only acquire knowledge but also develop values, habits, and relationships that can shape their future. However, one of the major challenges many teenagers face in this environment is navigating issues related to discipline, bullying, and the enforcement of school rules. These three elements deeply affect their emotional well-being, sense of safety, and motivation to learn.

1. Discipline or Disconnection?

Discipline is essential for maintaining order and promoting responsibility, but many young people today perceive discipline as harsh, unfair. In some schools, discipline is still punitive rather than restorative. Teenagers are often punished for misbehavior without being given the chance to explain their actions or learn from their mistakes.

Many teens act out because of deeper issues; family conflict, emotional trauma, or feelings of rejection. If school discipline ignores these underlying causes and only focuses on punishment, it risks pushing teenagers further away instead of pulling them toward positive change. What many teens truly need is understanding, mentoring, and boundaries guided by love and respect.

In Christian perspective, discipline should be rooted in love. Hebrews 12:6 says, *"For whom the Lord loves He chastens."* God's discipline aims to restore and guide, not to condemn or alienate. Schools, especially Christian ones, should aim to reflect this verse; correcting behavior while preserving dignity and helping students grow in character.

2. The Silent Crisis of Bullying

Bullying remains one of the most painful challenges for teenagers. It can take many forms; physical aggression, verbal abuse, social exclusion, or cyberbullying. Some teenagers endure daily torment that leaves deep emotional scars, affecting self-esteem, and even their faith in others.

What makes bullying so damaging is that it often happens in secret, away from teachers and adults. Victims may be too afraid to speak out. Some feel that reporting it would make them appear weak or lead to more attacks. Others have spoken up but were not taken seriously or were told to "just ignore it."

As a result, many teenagers suffer in silence. They may withdraw, become anxious or depressed, or even consider self-harm. The Church and community must recognize the spiritual weight of this issue. Jesus said in Matthew 25:40, *"Assuredly, I say to you, inasmuch as you did it to one of the least of these My brethren, you did it to Me."* Bullying offends the heart of God because it targets the vulnerable.

Schools must implement clear anti-bullying policies, but more importantly, they need to create a culture of compassion and accountability. Teenagers should be encouraged to stand up for one another, bullies should be punished, and they also should be helped to understand the damage they cause and turn away from such behavior.

3. When Rules Feel Like Chains

Every school needs rules to function well. These rules are designed to promote safety, respect, and learning. However, some teenagers struggle with rules that seem outdated, inconsistent, or overly rigid. For example, some schools have dress codes that target specific groups, rules about phone use that ignore how technology is a part of modern learning, or disciplinary measures that feel excessive for small mistakes.

Teenagers naturally begin to question rules as they seek identity and independence. This is part of growing up. The problem arises when their questions are met with dismissal instead of dialogue. When rules are applied without grace or flexibility, students feel oppressed rather than guided.

In some schools, teachers or administrators misuse rules to assert power rather than serve the students. This creates resentment and a breakdown of trust. When a teenager doesn't feel heard or valued, they are less likely to follow rules, even good ones.

As adults, we must remember that Jesus Christ, though a teacher and leader, was never legalistic. He corrected with compassion and taught in ways that connected deeply with people's real lives. Christian educators and parents must ask: Are our rules helping or hindering spiritual and emotional growth? Are we raising rule-followers or Christ-followers, those who live by principle and love?

4. How the Church Can Help

Many teenagers do not have a safe place to talk about what they go through in school. Youth ministries and Bible study groups can become those safe places. When the Church provides mentorship, open conversations, and prayer support, it gives teenagers tools to face these issues without losing their faith or confidence.

The Church can also work with schools and families to advocate for better systems; where discipline is fair, bullying is addressed seriously, and rules make room for grace. Teaching young people about identity in Christ, forgiveness, courage, and love can empower them to both resist negative peer pressure and be a voice for change.

Let us remember: Jesus Christ spent time with the outcast, the overlooked, and the hurting. When we take time to listen to teenagers and walk with them through their struggles at school, we reflect Christ' love and fulfill our calling.

Chapter 5

Challenges with Money

5.1 Financial Illiteracy

One of the most pressing and often overlooked challenges facing teenagers today is financial illiteracy. While young people are growing up in a world filled with digital transactions, online banking, and endless opportunities for spending, many lack even the most basic understanding of how money works. This puts them at risk of falling into poor financial habits, debt, and a cycle of mismanagement.

The Root of the Problem

Most schools still do not include practical financial education in their curriculum. Teenagers learn about history, science, and mathematics, but rarely are they taught how to budget, save, invest, or manage credit.

As a result, many young people enter adulthood without a foundation in financial decision-making. Some don't know how to read a bank statement, how interest works, or what a budget looks like.

Many teens today also grow up in homes where financial struggles are common. If their parents or guardians are also financially illiterate or struggling to make ends meet, the cycle continues. In such households, conversations about money might be filled with fear, secrecy, or stress. Instead of learning positive financial habits, these teens absorb anxiety, confusion, or avoidance when it comes to money matters.

The Rise of the "Spend Culture"

Another influence contributing to teenage financial illiteracy is the strong *consumer culture* that targets young people. Social media influencers, online advertisements, and peer pressure often encourage teens to buy the latest clothes, gadgets, and digital products; even when they cannot afford them. In this "spend culture," having the newest phone or brand-name shoes becomes a way to gain approval or feel successful.

Yet, this culture creates unrealistic expectations about money. Teenagers may begin to equate happiness and identity with material possessions. This mindset can lead to reckless spending, borrowing money without understanding the consequences, or feeling inferior because they cannot keep up with wealthier peers.

Some teens even get involved in risky behaviors to make quick money. They may engage in online scams, illegal activities, or manipulative relationships just to afford the lifestyle they see others flaunting online. Without a strong understanding of money's purpose and power, they become vulnerable to dangerous shortcuts.

Consequences of Financial Illiteracy

When teenagers do not understand how money works, the consequences can be long-lasting:

- *Debt accumulation*: Teenagers who start using credit cards or buy-now-pay-later services without knowing how interest works may quickly fall into debt.

- *Lack of savings*: Many do not see the need to save or invest early, missing the opportunity to build a secure financial future.

- *Financial stress*: Even at a young age, teens can experience anxiety over money, especially if they are expected to contribute to the household or fend for themselves.

- *Poor choices*: Financial illiteracy can lead to poor decisions in choosing student loans, jobs, or managing income from part-time work.

- *Vulnerability to exploitation*: Teens who do not understand financial systems are more likely to be taken advantage of in the workplace or online.

What Can Be Done?

Addressing financial illiteracy among teenagers requires a collective effort from families, schools, churches, and communities.

1. Education at School and Home

Schools should prioritize basic financial education. Courses should teach students how to budget, plan for expenses, understand taxes, and think long-term about financial goals. Parents and guardians should also talk to their teens openly about money; explaining how bills are paid, how savings work, and why it is important to avoid unnecessary debt.

2. Teaching Biblical Financial Principles

Churches and faith-based organizations can play a major role by teaching biblical principles of money. The Bible speaks about stewardship, contentment, diligence, and generosity. When teenagers understand that money is a tool, it helps reshape their mindset. Scriptures like Proverbs 21:20 (*"There is desirable treasure, and oil in the dwelling of the wise, but a foolish man squanders it"*) can be powerful guides.

3. Promoting Entrepreneurship and Saving Culture

Teens should be encouraged to earn money in honest ways; through small jobs, summer work, or creating products and services. They should be taught how to save a portion of their earnings, give generously, and wisely invest. This builds responsibility and helps them see the value of work.

4. Using Technology Wisely

There are many apps and tools designed to help people track spending, budget, and set financial goals. Teenagers are already comfortable with technology, why not teach them how to use it for financial growth instead of just for spending?

Financial illiteracy is a silent crisis among teenagers today. As they face more financial pressure and exposure than any previous generation, they must be equipped with knowledge, wisdom, and values to manage money well. Without this, they risk repeating the mistakes of previous generations, falling into new traps created by a fast-changing financial world.

Empowering teens with financial education is not just about helping them avoid debt, it's about preparing them to be wise stewards, responsible adults, and future leaders who will use money as a tool to serve God, help others, and build a better future.

5.2 Peer Pressure and Materialism

In today's hyper-connected world, teenagers are under constant pressure to look, act, and live a certain way. One of the most powerful forces shaping their relationship with money is peer pressure combined with materialism. This combination often leads young people to desire things not out of necessity, but out of a deep need to belong, to be admired, or to appear successful in the eyes of others.

The Influence of Friends and Social Media

Teenagers naturally desire acceptance. Friendships are central to their lives, and the fear of rejection or ridicule can make them vulnerable to peer influence. When a teen's friends wear expensive clothes, use the latest smartphones, or constantly talk about the "next big thing," it creates an invisible standard that others feel they must meet to be accepted.

On top of peer influence is the massive pressure from *social media platforms*. Instagram, TikTok, and Snapchat bombard teenagers with curated images of what seems like perfect lives. Influencers, celebrities, and even classmates showcase luxury items, trendy outfits, international vacations, and flashy lifestyles. Many teens begin to compare themselves with what they see and feel they are "less than" if they cannot keep up.

This comparison quickly leads to materialism, a belief that owning certain things will make them more valuable, more respected, or happier. But the truth is, materialism is a trap. It creates a cycle of constant wanting, temporary satisfaction, and long-term emptiness.

The Cost of Keeping Up

To maintain an image that fits in or stands out, some teens begin to make unwise financial decisions. They may:

- Spend all their allowance or part-time job income on clothes, shoes, or gadgets they don't need.

- Pressure their parents into buying things they cannot afford.

- Fall into envy or low self-worth when they cannot match others.

- Engage in risky or dishonest behaviors to get money quickly.

- Neglect long-term goals like saving or studying just to maintain appearances.

Some teens even develop an unhealthy view of success, believing it only comes through money and material possessions, rather than through character, skills, or purpose.

What Teens Really Need

Behind the desire for material things is often a deeper need: to be *seen, valued, and affirmed.* When teenagers feel secure in their identity, loved by God, and supported by a strong community, they are far less likely to seek validation through things.

Teenagers must be taught that value does not come from what they wear, drive, or post online, but from who they are in Christ. Romans 12:2 reminds us: *"Do not be conformed to this world, but be transformed by the renewing of your mind."* This scripture is a call to resist worldly pressure and live by Kingdom values.

Building a Healthy Identity and View of Money

To help teens overcome peer pressure and materialism, parents, teachers, and spiritual leaders should:

- *Affirm Their Identity in Christ*
  Teach teens that they are fearfully and wonderfully made (Psalm 139:14) and that their worth is not for sale.

- *Model Contentment*
  Adults should demonstrate how to be content with what they have, live within their means, and avoid the trap of comparison.

- *Celebrate Non-Material Achievements*
  Praise teens for their kindness, creativity, hard work, and integrity, not just their appearance or possessions.

- *Create Safe Spaces for Conversation*
  Let teens talk about the pressures they face and help them process what is true, what is hype, and what really matters.

- *Disciple Them in Stewardship*
  Teach teens that money is a gift and a tool. Help them see how it can be used to glorify God, bless others, and prepare for the future.

Peer pressure and materialism are real forces that shape how teenagers handle money and how they see themselves. But when teens are grounded in God's Word, surrounded by healthy influences, and taught to value what truly lasts, they can rise above the pressures of the world. Instead of living to impress, they can live to express the love and wisdom of God even in how they handle money.

5.3 Teen Work, Hustle Culture, and Future Fears

The world of today's teenager is fast-paced, highly digital, and filled with both new opportunities and mounting pressures. One of the most complex shifts in recent years is the growing emphasis on productivity, side hustles, and future security. Young people are being pulled into the economic world earlier than ever, not just to earn money for basic needs or wants, but because of a deeper, often unspoken fear about their future. Let's unpack this cultural moment and its spiritual implications.

The Rise of Teen Hustle Culture

"Hustle culture" is a term often used to describe a lifestyle where constant work, productivity, and busyness are glorified. It's no longer just about getting a part-time job after school; many teenagers today feel the need to be entrepreneurs, content creators, influencers, or online sellers, all while managing school, social life, and family responsibilities. While working and developing life skills can be positive, the motivation behind this movement is often rooted in anxiety rather than inspiration.

Social media platforms play a major role in this shift. Teenagers scroll through endless posts of their peers starting small businesses, selling handmade crafts, promoting affiliate links, or building social media brands. They are constantly exposed to others' "success stories" that glamorize financial independence at an early age. This creates an atmosphere where teens feel they are falling behind if they are not also working, earning, or planning their financial future aggressively.

Why Are Teens So Concerned About Money?

Several reasons fuel this concern:

- *Economic Uncertainty:* Teenagers today are more aware of financial instability than previous generations. They see their parents struggle with bills, jobs, or the rising cost of living. They've heard stories of adults who worked hard yet are still in debt. The future doesn't feel secure, and the message many receive is: "You're on your own."

- *Student Loan Anxiety:* Higher education is expensive. Even in countries where tuition is subsidized, the cost of living, textbooks, and transportation adds up. Teens fear debt, and some start saving or working early to prepare. Others are rethinking whether college is even worth it.

- *The Pressure to "Make It" Early:* In this era, success is expected to come fast. At 16 or 17, many teens feel like they should already have a clear vision, a profitable project, or even a digital portfolio before they've even truly started adult life.

The Emotional Toll

This obsession with work, money, and future planning takes a toll on the teenage soul. It creates:

- *Stress and burnout:* Many teens don't sleep enough, don't rest properly, and feel guilty when they take a break. Even during school holidays, the pressure to "use the time well" is intense.

- *Loss of childhood joy:* Hustle culture robs young people of simple pleasures. Many teens forget how to be kids. They stop playing, exploring, and imagining because their minds are filled with financial goals.

- *Spiritual numbness:* When performance and achievement become idols, there's little room left for God. The still small voice of the Holy Spirit is drowned out by the noise of comparison and self-reliance.

What Does the Bible Say?

The Bible encourages hard work and diligence but warns against anxiety about the future. Jesus said in Matthew 6:34, *'Therefore do not worry about tomorrow, for tomorrow will worry about its own things. Sufficient for the day is its own trouble."* This does not mean teens shouldn't plan or work, but rather, their hearts should be anchored in God, not in fear of the unknown.

Colossians 3:23 reminds us, *"And whatever you do, do it heartily, as to the Lord and not to men."* Teen work and creativity can be acts of worship when done in the right spirit. But when hustling becomes a way to earn value, prove identity, or escape fear, it leads down a dangerous path.

Proverbs 3:5-6 teaches a vital truth for this generation: *"Trust in the Lord with all your heart, and lean not on your own understanding; in all your ways acknowledge Him, and He shall direct your paths."*

Teens need to know: Your value does not come from your productivity. You are not behind. You are not late. You are loved by God, and He has a plan for your life, even if you don't have it all figured out.

How the Church Can Help

Church communities must rise to guide teens through this confusing season. Here are a few ways we can help:

- *Provide Biblical Financial Teaching:* Many teens have never heard a sermon or teaching about money from a Godly perspective. Churches can hold youth seminars on budgeting, contentment, giving, and faith for provision.

- *Encourage Sabbath Rest:* Teach teens the power of rest. Remind them that it's not laziness to stop and recharge. It's obedience to God and good stewardship of their mental health.

- *Promote Kingdom Identity:* Help teens build identity in Christ, not in what they own or achieve. Celebrate their character, not just their performance.

- *Create Opportunities to Serve and Grow:* If teens want to work, channel that energy into missions. Let them use their talents to serve others; help in media teams, church businesses, and youth outreaches. Redirect hustle into purpose.

- *Offer Counseling and Mentorship:* Not every teenager wants to admit they're afraid. Many look confident but are deeply anxious about their future. One-on-one mentorship can help them process these fears in a safe environment.

A Final Word to the Teen Reader

If you're a teenager reading this book: You don't have to figure everything out today. It's okay to dream and work hard, but don't carry the world on your shoulders. That's not your job, it's God's. Seek Him first. He knows the plans He has for you, and they are good plans.

Let your work be joyful, not burdensome. Let your future be full of faith, not fear. And let your value be rooted in God's love, not in your hustle.

Chapter 6

Emotional and Mental Health Struggles

6.1 Anxiety, Depression, and Loneliness

The teenage years are a time of intense emotional and mental development. It is a season of exploration, identity formation, peer pressure, and exposure to countless influences. In today's world, teenagers are facing emotional and mental health challenges at an alarming rate. Among these, anxiety, depression, and loneliness stand out as the silent battles many teenagers fight daily, often without the knowledge of their parents, teachers, or even close friends.

Anxiety: A Constant Internal Alarm

Anxiety is more than just being nervous before an exam or feeling tense about a social situation. For many teenagers, it is a persistent state of worry, fear, or unease that disrupts their ability to function normally. The pressure to perform well in school, be accepted by peers, look a certain way, or meet family expectations often becomes overwhelming. Social media, instead of being a place of fun and connection, can turn into a constant source of comparison and self-doubt. Teenagers begin to believe they are not enough, not pretty enough, not smart enough, not talented enough.

This can lead to physical symptoms such as sleeplessness, headaches, digestive issues, and panic. When left unaddressed, anxiety can affect a teenager's academic performance, social life, and even their spiritual walk. It is important for parents, guardians, and spiritual leaders to be watchful and approachable. A simple question like, *"How are you really doing?"* asked in love, can open the door to healing.

Depression: The Hidden Pain

Depression among teenagers is also on the rise. Unlike temporary sadness, depression is a deep and long-lasting sense of hopelessness, emptiness, and disinterest in life. A teenager who is depressed might seem constantly tired, uninterested in activities they once enjoyed, irritable, or withdrawn.

This darkness often goes unnoticed because some teenagers become experts at hiding their emotions. They smile in public, attend church, and act "normal" while silently crying out for help. Depression does not always have a clear cause. Sometimes it is linked to trauma, bullying, family problems, academic stress, or spiritual emptiness. But at other times, it seems to appear out of nowhere.

The Church has an essential role to play in helping teenagers walk through depression. Preaching hope, encouraging open conversations, praying for deliverance, and connecting teens with Godly counselors or mentors can save lives. We must provide a safe environment where healing can begin.

Loneliness: Alone in a Crowd

Ironically, many teenagers today feel deeply alone; even though they are constantly connected to hundreds of people online. Loneliness is not just about being physically alone; it's the aching feeling of being unseen, unloved, and misunderstood. In schools, churches, and homes, some teenagers walk around unnoticed, with no one truly listening to their hearts.

Family breakdown, constant movement, absent parents, and busy schedules have contributed to the emotional disconnection many teens feel. At times, they seek connection in the wrong places: unhealthy relationships, substance abuse, or gangs. Others retreat into isolation, spending hours on their phones or gaming, hoping to numb the emptiness they feel inside.

The Bible reminds us in **Psalm 68:6** that *"God sets the solitary in families."* The Church can be that family, a place where teenagers feel loved, valued, and accepted. Every teenager needs at least one adult who listens, mentors, and shows consistent love. Every youth ministry should be built not just on entertainment or sermons, but on relationships that reflect the heart of Jesus.

Responding as a Church and Society

The emotional and mental health struggles of teenagers should concern all of us: parents, educators, spiritual leaders, and policymakers. Mental health is not a worldly concept to be ignored by the Church. Jesus came to heal the brokenhearted and set the captives free (Luke 4:18). This includes emotional and mental bondage.

Here are a few ways we can respond:

- *Prayer and Intercession:* The enemy seeks to destroy the minds of the youth. Let us cover our teenagers in prayer daily, that their minds be renewed and protected by the Word of God.

- *Education and Awareness:* Teach parents, pastors, and teachers about the signs of emotional distress. Understanding leads to compassion.

- *Safe Spaces:* Create environments where teens can talk honestly without judgment. Group discussions, counseling, and peer support programs in churches can make a difference.

- *Godly Mentorship:* Encourage spiritual mothers and fathers to walk closely with teens. Many just need someone to say, *"I believe in you."*

- *Professional Help When Needed:* Sometimes, prayer must be combined with therapy or medical support. This is not a lack of faith, but wisdom. God can use Christian counselors and medical professionals to bring healing.

A Message of Hope to the Teenager

If you are a teenager reading this and you are struggling with anxiety, depression, or loneliness, know this: ***you are not alone***. Jesus sees you. He knows your name. He cares about every tear and every thought. You are not weird, broken, or forgotten. You are loved beyond measure.

Don't be afraid to speak up. Talk to your parents, a pastor, a teacher, or a trusted adult. Reach out for help. You are not weak for needing support, it is strength to face your battles and not hide. God is with you, and He will bring you through. Your life has a purpose, and your future is bright.

6.2 Self-Esteem and Body Image Issues

In a world driven by curated online identities, filtered photos, and impossible beauty standards, many teens struggle to accept and appreciate themselves as they are. What they see in the mirror often becomes a battlefield of comparison, self-doubt, and emotional pain.

The Influence of Social Media

Social media platforms like Instagram, TikTok, and Snapchat bombard teenagers with images of "perfect" bodies and lifestyles. Celebrities, influencers, and even peers seem to live flawless lives, flaunting toned bodies, fashionable clothes, glowing skin, and constant excitement. Teenagers, still developing their sense of identity, often internalize these images, believing that they must look or live the same way to be accepted or loved.

This constant exposure creates a false reality. What they see is usually filtered, edited, or staged. But teenagers rarely understand the full extent of this deception. Instead, they compare their real, everyday selves to idealized online personas and come up short. This comparison leads to a distorted self-image and declining self-worth.

Girls may feel pressured to be slim, curvy in the "right" places, and always stylish. Boys may feel they need to be muscular, tall, and dominant. Those who do not fit these molds may feel unattractive or invisible. The result is an emotional wound that cuts deep and often silently.

The Role of Peer Pressure

Beyond social media, peer pressure in schools and social circles also fuels self-esteem struggles. Teenagers often feel judged by how they look, dress, or act. Those who are overweight, underweight, have acne, wear second-hand clothes, or simply look different may face teasing or exclusion.

Name-calling, bullying, are sadly common. Some teens are mocked for having braces, being too tall or too short, wearing glasses, or simply being different from the group's definition of "cool." This can lead to deep embarrassment, self-isolation, and depression.

In response, many teenagers try to change themselves through excessive dieting, over-exercising, or using unsafe beauty products, to fit in. Others retreat emotionally, hiding their real feelings behind jokes, sarcasm, or silence.

Internal Battles

While the outside pressures are real, the internal voice can be even more brutal. Many teens develop a harsh inner critic that constantly tells them they are not good enough, attractive enough, or worthy of love. This negative self-talk can become a soundtrack playing over and over in their minds.

Over time, this damages not just how they see themselves physically but also how they view their entire worth. Self-esteem is more than skin deep; it touches every area of a teenager's life. A teen who feels unattractive may not just dislike their body but may also begin to believe they have nothing valuable to contribute in school, friendships, or their future.

Low self-esteem affects how they make decisions, set goals, take risks, and relate to others. It can keep them from speaking up in class, trying out for a sport, or making new friends. Some may even settle for unhealthy relationships because they believe they don't deserve better.

The Church's Response

The Church must be a place of healing. Teenagers need to hear from their spiritual leaders that their worth is not in their waistline, skin tone, or hairstyle but in their identity as children of God. **Psalm 139:14** reminds us, *"I will praise You, for I am fearfully and wonderfully made; marvelous are Your works, and that my soul knows very well."*

When teenagers internalize the truth that they are made in God's image and loved unconditionally, their sense of worth begins to heal. The Church should teach these truths clearly and repeatedly, creating a safe space where teens can be honest about their struggles without fear of judgment.

We must go beyond sermons and organize youth gatherings, mentorship sessions, and support groups that focus on mental health, self-esteem, and identity in Christ. When teenagers see their value through God's eyes, the lies of society begin to lose their power.

What Parents and Mentors Can Do

Parents, guardians, and mentors play a critical role in shaping a teenager's self-image. Encouragement, affirmation, and genuine interest in their lives make a massive difference. Instead of focusing on appearances, we should highlight character, talents, and growth.

Speak words of life over your teen. Compliment their kindness, their effort, and their creativity. Be careful not to compare them with others, especially siblings or cousins. Instead, celebrate their uniqueness.

Also, be watchful of signs of emotional distress. If your teenager avoids mirrors, refuses to eat, complains constantly about their looks, or shows signs of depression, don't ignore it. Listen with love, offer support, and don't hesitate to seek professional help if needed.

Let them know their worth is not tied to how others see them, but to how God sees them, and He sees them as His masterpiece.

A Message to Teenagers

Dear Teenager,

You may not feel like it, but you are beautiful, just as you are. Your body may not look like the ones on Instagram, but it is strong, capable, and created by God Himself. Don't let the world tell you that you are less than because of how you look. You are more than your skin, more than your weight, more than your likes and followers.

Look into the mirror and remind yourself:

"I am loved.

I am valuable.

I am enough."

Surround yourself with those who uplift you, not those who bring you down. Don't be afraid to speak to someone you trust when you're struggling. It is normal to seek help. Your feelings are valid, and your healing is possible.

And remember this: God does not make mistakes. You are His design, His joy, and His treasure. The more you see yourself through His eyes, the more you'll discover the strength, beauty, and confidence already inside you.

6.3 Comparison Culture

In today's digital world, teenagers are more connected than ever, but not necessarily more fulfilled. One of the greatest emotional and mental health challenges facing this generation is the trap of comparison culture. Social media, peer competition, societal expectations, and even the pressures within family structures have created an invisible but powerful force that constantly pushes young people to measure their worth against others.

From the moment they wake up, many teenagers scroll through social media feeds filled with carefully curated images of other people's "perfect" lives. They see friends traveling, influencers flaunting new clothes, students celebrating awards, or peers posing with their ideal body types. What's often missed is that these images are edited, filtered, and sometimes entirely fabricated. Yet, the subconscious message teenagers receive is clear: *You are not enough unless you measure up.*

The Identity Crisis

Comparison culture leads teenagers into an identity crisis. Instead of learning who they truly are, they begin to shape themselves based on who others appear to be. They try to imitate fashion trends, adopt certain behaviors, or even change their values in an attempt to be accepted or admired. When they don't get the same number of likes, followers, or compliments, they don't feel good.

This constant evaluation can lead to low self-esteem, anxiety, and even depression. A teenager who gets good grades may suddenly feel inadequate because another peer scored just a few points higher and shared it online. A young girl who once felt beautiful may question her worth because she doesn't look like the influencers she follows. Boys may compare their athletic abilities or popularity and start to feel inferior.

The issue is not competition in itself; healthy competition can be motivating. The danger lies in the comparison that is rooted in *insecurity* and *false perceptions.* Unlike healthy competition, which can inspire self-improvement, unhealthy comparison breeds jealousy and self-hate.

The Role of Technology

Technology has amplified this culture. Before the internet, comparison was mostly limited to classmates or neighborhood friends. Now, a teenager in Africa can compare their lifestyle with someone in America, Asia, or Europe, often forgetting the vast differences in context and opportunity.

Moreover, the rise of "influencer culture" has made it seem as if success is measured by appearance, possessions, or popularity.

Teenagers are subtly taught that if they do not look, act, or achieve like those they follow, they are less valuable. This mindset creates pressure to perform instead of grow, and to impress rather than express.

The Danger of Hidden Pain

Comparison culture doesn't just affect what teenagers think about themselves; it also shapes how they treat others. A teen who constantly feels behind may start to resent others who seem more successful. This can lead to bullying, gossip, or passive aggression. Others withdraw, isolate themselves, or pretend to be someone they're not just to fit in.

Even more concerning is that many teenagers suffer in silence. They wear smiles, post selfies, and join in trends, but deep down, they are overwhelmed by feelings of inadequacy. They think, *"Why can't I be like them?"* or *"What's wrong with me?"* And because everyone else also appears to be doing fine, they believe they are the only ones struggling.

How Can We Help?

As parents, pastors, teachers, and leaders, we must address comparison culture with wisdom, empathy, and truth. First, we must remind teenagers of their God-given identity. Every teenager is uniquely created in the image of God, with specific gifts, purposes, and timing. Psalm 139:14 says, *"I praise You because I am fearfully and wonderfully made."* This truth must be rooted deep in their hearts.

Second, we must educate them on the reality behind what they see online. Helping them understand that social media is not real life can remove the sting of comparison. Teach them to appreciate what they have while celebrating others without feeling threatened.

Third, create open conversations about mental health and emotions. Let them know they are not alone. When teenagers feel heard and seen, healing begins.

Lastly, we must model contentment and authenticity in our own lives. Adults who constantly compare themselves to others, whether it's about money, ministry, family, or status, send a message that comparison is normal and acceptable. When we demonstrate gratitude, humility, and confidence in God's timing, we become examples of freedom.

Comparison culture is one of the silent destroyers of teenage confidence, joy, and peace. But it can be overcome. When teenagers learn to value who they are, grow at their own pace, and cheer others on without losing themselves, they rise above the noise. In a world screaming, *"Be like them!"*, they can stand and say, *"I choose to be who God made me to be."*

Chapter 7

Family Conflict and Misunderstanding

7.1 Broken Homes, Strict Parenting, or Neglect

Family is meant to be a place of love, understanding, and support. But for many teenagers today, home has become a battleground of conflict, silence, or misunderstanding. The family unit, once the stronghold of stability, has increasingly been shaken by divorce, absentee parenting, extreme control, or complete emotional neglect. These challenges do not just affect the family dynamics; they deeply shape the teenager's identity, emotional health, and future choices.

Broken Homes

A "broken home" refers to a family where the parents are separated, divorced, or one or both are absent. While not every separated family creates a negative environment, the lack of unity, peace, and presence of both parents often leaves deep scars on teenagers. Many begin to ask questions like:

- *Why did this happen?*

- *Was it my fault?*

- *Who do I belong to?*

Children from broken homes may find themselves caught in the middle of arguments, used as messengers or emotional pawns between parents. They may have to constantly move between two houses, adapt to different rules, or feel torn between loyalty to both parents. This instability often results in insecurity, anger, and withdrawal. Some teens rebel openly, while others suffer silently with depression, anxiety, or confusion about relationships and trust.

Teenagers in broken homes need assurance that they are not the cause of the family breakdown. They need mentors, spiritual leaders, and caregivers who can step in with consistent love, guidance, and support. The Church can become a healing community for them, offering them the family environment they long for, filled with acceptance, purpose, and hope.

Strict Parenting

While discipline is necessary, strict or authoritarian parenting often leads to fear-based obedience and rebellion rather than respect. Teenagers raised in homes where there is no room for honest dialogue, self-expression, or grace often feel suffocated. They may begin to live a double life, outwardly conforming while inwardly rebelling.

Strict parenting often comes from fear; parents wanting to protect their children from the dangers of the world. But without balance, this approach can backfire. Rules without relationship often result in resentment. Teens want to be heard, understood, and given space to grow. They need guidance, not just commands; they need to be taught *why*, not just *what*.

When parents fail to listen, teens turn to peers, online communities, or even strangers who seem to "get them." Sadly, many fall into the wrong hands because no one at home was willing to hear them out.

Parenting teenagers in today's complex world requires wisdom, patience, and most of all, love. Correction must be balanced with compassion. Parents must learn to walk with their teens through their questions and mistakes, not just stand above them with rules.

Neglect

Neglect is perhaps the most silent and damaging form of family conflict. A teenager who is ignored, emotionally abandoned, or left to raise themselves will struggle to feel worthy, loved, or significant. Neglect can be physical: lack of food, care, or supervision, or emotional: no words of affirmation, no attention, no interest in the teen's life.

In some homes, parents are too busy with work, distracted by their own problems, or absent due to travel or abandonment. The teen learns to survive alone. They make decisions based on trial and error. They raise themselves emotionally, spiritually, and mentally. Over time, this independence may look like strength, but it often hides deep loneliness and pain.

Emotionally neglected teens may act out to get attention, or they may isolate themselves completely. They may also become people-pleasers, constantly seeking approval from others to fill the void of parental love. As a result, they are vulnerable to bad influences, abusive relationships, and addictions.

The role of the Church and community becomes vital here. Ministries that provide mentorship, youth programs, and spiritual parenting can fill some of the gaps left by neglect. Youth leaders, teachers, and volunteers can become the listening ears, encouraging voices, and wise counsel that these teens need.

Family conflict is a major contributor to the emotional and spiritual struggles of today's teenagers. Whether through broken homes, strict parenting, or neglect, many teens carry invisible wounds that affect how they see themselves and the world. But these wounds are not the end of the story. With love, intentional relationships, and God's grace, healing is possible. The Church must rise up to become the family many teenagers are missing; a place where they are seen, known, and loved.

7.2 Communication Breakdown

One of the most significant sources of conflict between teenagers and their families is a breakdown in communication. As teenagers grow and begin to discover who they are, they often struggle to express their thoughts and emotions. At the same time, parents may find it difficult to understand their child's changing needs, behavior, and attitude. This mutual frustration, if not addressed, can lead to ongoing misunderstandings, emotional distance, and even open conflict in the home.

The Changing Language of Teenagers

Teenagers often develop their own way of speaking; slang, online expressions, and indirect ways of saying what they truly feel. For many parents, this new "language" can feel like a barrier. What a teenager says and what they mean may be two different things. For example, when a teen says:

"You don't understand me," it may actually mean, "I need you to listen to me without judging."

When they say, "Leave me alone," they may actually be crying out for attention, connection, or a moment of peace.

Parents, on the other hand, may speak in a more direct, corrective tone, which teenagers can interpret as controlling, insensitive, or even hostile. A simple instruction like "Clean your room" might trigger a defensive reaction if the teenager feels that their autonomy is being threatened. The result is that both sides feel unheard and disrespected.

The Emotional Gap

Teenagers are often emotionally intense and reactive. Their brains are still developing, especially the parts responsible for regulating emotions and thinking logically. Because of this, their responses to situations may seem exaggerated or irrational to adults. But for the teen, their feelings are very real. If a parent responds with criticism, sarcasm, or indifference, it only deepens the emotional gap.

On the other side, parents are dealing with stress from work, finances, and other adult responsibilities. They may not always have the patience or emotional energy to decode what their teenager is trying to say or to sit and listen when there's a busy schedule ahead. When communication becomes rushed, dismissive, or reactive, it sends a signal to the teen that their voice doesn't matter. Over time, this can result in silence or rebellion.

Common Communication Traps in Families

- *Interrupting and Not Listening*: Both parents and teens are guilty of this. When conversations turn into arguments, people often stop listening in order to defend their point of view.

- *Speaking with Assumptions*: Parents may assume they know why their child is acting a certain way without asking. Teens may also assume their parents will not understand or care.

- *Passive Communication*: Some teenagers avoid conflict by keeping everything inside, pretending that nothing is wrong. This silence may look like obedience but often hides pain, resentment, or confusion.

- *Aggressive Responses:* Shouting, blaming, or threatening language shuts down any chance for healthy dialogue. Teenagers may copy this behavior or become withdrawn.

- *Digital Distraction:* Modern communication is deeply affected by phones and screens. Parents and teenagers may live under the same roof but barely talk because each is glued to their devices.

Restoring Communication in the Home

The good news is that communication can be restored. Even small changes can rebuild trust and improve the emotional climate of the family. Here are some practical steps:

- **Create Safe Spaces for Talking**
  Families need intentional time where members can talk freely, without fear of judgment or punishment. This might be during dinner, in the car, or during a walk. The key is creating a regular rhythm of listening and sharing.

- **Practice Active Listening**
  This means listening with the goal of understanding, not correcting. When a teenager feels heard, they are more likely to open up and even accept guidance.

- **Validate Feelings Before Giving Advice**
  Instead of jumping into solutions, parents can first acknowledge what the teen feels. A statement like, "That sounds really frustrating," shows empathy and opens the door for a deeper conversation.

- *Teach Teens How to Express Themselves Clearly*
  Teenagers also need to learn how to express their needs respectfully. This might mean using "I feel" statements instead of accusations. For example,

  "I feel hurt when I'm not allowed to explain" is better than "You never listen!"

- *Put Away Devices During Family Moments*
  Having tech-free zones or times can help everyone be more present and engaged. Even one hour of focused time can make a big difference.

The Role of the Church and Community

Churches and youth ministries can play a key role in bridging the communication gap between parents and teenagers. Workshops, parenting classes, and youth counseling can equip both sides with tools for better understanding. Sometimes, a neutral voice from a pastor, mentor, or youth leader can help interpret what a teenager is trying to express and guide the family toward healing.

Communication is the lifeline of any relationship. When it breaks down, love and respect begin to suffer. But when families choose to rebuild it, through listening, empathy, and intentional connection, many conflicts and misunderstandings can be resolved.

The teenage years do not have to be years of distance. With God's help and a commitment to healthy dialogue, families can grow even stronger through these years.

7.3 Teens Raising Themselves

In many homes today, a silent issue is unfolding: teenagers raising themselves. Whether due to parental absence, neglect, emotional unavailability, or the harsh demands of survival in broken families, more and more young people are navigating life largely on their own. This self-parenting comes at a cost: emotionally, mentally, and spiritually, and it is often hidden behind a mask of independence or defiance.

The Reality of the "Absent Parent"

Some teens are effectively raising themselves because one or both parents are physically absent, due to work abroad, separation, divorce, or abandonment. In other cases, parents are present in the home but absent in the relationship. They may be too busy, too stressed, or too emotionally disconnected to provide meaningful guidance or consistent support. In such situations, teenagers become their own disciplinarians, decision-makers, and counselors.

Many youths wake up, go to school, manage their meals, and return home without anyone checking in on them. Some must care for younger siblings or even their own children. Without boundaries, structure, or parental encouragement, these teens are forced to become adults too soon, navigating critical life choices without wisdom or protection.

The Pain Behind the Mask

While some teens may appear strong, rebellious, or self-sufficient, the truth is that most are simply surviving. They long for affection, correction, and affirmation, but they have learned not to expect it. Often, these teens experience deep loneliness. They may struggle with self-worth, anxiety, or fear.

The pain of rejection or neglect can lead to dangerous coping mechanisms. Without healthy parental involvement, many teens turn to social media, unhealthy friendships, intimate relationships, or substance use to fill the emotional void. In essence, they are seeking guidance, love, and structure that should have come from their home.

We must understand that raising oneself does not mean a teenager is doing well. It often means they are wounded, overwhelmed, and vulnerable to exploitation or poor decisions.

The Role of the Church and Mentors

The Church can step into this gap with grace and love. We must recognize the teens in our communities who are functionally raising themselves and offer consistent mentorship, accountability, and care. Every local Church should have a vision to adopt these young people spiritually and emotionally, helping them to understand that God sees them, values them, and has not left them to survive alone.

Paul said in 1 Corinthians 4:15, *"For though you might have ten thousand instructors in Christ, yet you do not have many fathers."* Many teens today do not need more instructions. They need spiritual fathers and mothers who will walk with them patiently, affirm their worth, and gently guide them into purpose.

Even small actions, checking in regularly, offering encouragement, and inviting them into family spaces, can make a huge difference. A teen who feels seen and valued is less likely to fall into despair or rebellion.

Raising Themselves Spiritually

Interestingly, many teenagers who raise themselves physically also try to raise themselves spiritually. Without spiritual leadership at home, they explore their faith on their own, often through internet preachers, podcasts, or fragments of truth picked up along the way. Some develop strong convictions early, while others are confused, mixing worldly ideologies with spiritual hunger.

Here, the Church must again be present, offering sound doctrine, a space to ask questions, and a loving environment where they can grow in Christ. Discipleship should be practical and personal. These teens need even more than Sunday sermons; they need hands-on love, structured Bible studies, and mentorship that feels safe and secure.

Reparenting Through God's Love

There is hope for every teen who has had to raise themselves. Through Jesus Christ, the love of the Heavenly Father can heal the wounds of abandonment, rejection, and neglect. Psalm 27:10 says, *"Though my father and mother forsake me, the Lord will receive me."* God's heart beats for every young person who feels alone in the world.

We must teach teens that God's presence can become their home. His Word can become their compass. His Spirit can become their comforter and guide. As they encounter the perfect Father in heaven, they begin to unlearn lies and walk in restored identity.

However, this doesn't happen overnight. It requires a spiritual community, one that walks patiently with them, that believes in their potential even when they make mistakes, and that never gives up on them.

A Call to Action

We cannot stand by while a generation raises itself. Families must be challenged to rise again; to repent of passivity, to reconcile, and to reengage with their children.

Parents must be equipped with the tools to parent with love and wisdom. And where biological parents are missing or unable, the Church must step in with compassion, not condemnation.

Youth ministries must shift from entertainment to discipleship. Pastors and leaders must create space for raw conversations, healing prayers, and healthy family models. Every teenager deserves a safe place to grow; a place where they are known, heard, and led.

Let us not judge those who are raising themselves. Instead, let us ask:

- **Who can I mentor?**

- **Who can I father or mother in the Lord?**

- **Whose story can I change by simply showing up?**

The answer to the crisis of self-raised teens is not in systems alone, but in relationships filled with truth, grace, and the power of God's love.

Chapter 8

Peer Pressure and Substance Abuse

8.1 The Need to Fit In

One of the most powerful forces shaping the behavior and decisions of teenagers today is the **need to fit in**. This need is deeply rooted in human nature; we all crave acceptance, belonging, and validation from those around us.

For teenagers, this desire intensifies as they are in a critical stage of identity formation, social development, and emotional growth. Peer groups become a primary source of approval and a benchmark for what is "normal" or "cool." This drive to belong can sometimes push young people toward risky behaviors, including substance abuse.

The Social Landscape of Adolescence

Adolescence is a period of transition between childhood and adulthood, marked by rapid physical, emotional, and cognitive changes. Teenagers are discovering who they are and where they fit in society. At this stage, friends and peer groups often become more important than family. The opinions and actions of peers carry significant weight, influencing attitudes, self-esteem, and choices.

In many cases, teenagers find themselves in environments where the pressure to conform is intense. They may feel that to be accepted, they must dress a certain way, speak with a particular slang, or engage in behaviors that align with the group's values, even if these behaviors contradict their own instincts or values.

The Role of Peer Pressure

Peer pressure can be both explicit and subtle. It might come in the form of direct encouragement: "Come on, try this," "Everyone's doing it," or "If you don't, you're not one of us." Or it might be indirect, such as noticing that everyone else seems to be participating in certain activities, leaving the individual feeling isolated or invisible if they abstain.

For many teenagers, the fear of rejection or ridicule can outweigh their better judgment. The drive to avoid loneliness or exclusion is so strong that it can lead them to make decisions they otherwise wouldn't consider, especially when it comes to experimenting with substances like alcohol, tobacco, or drugs.

Substance Abuse as a Tool for Acceptance

Substance use often appears as a way for teenagers to "break the ice," bond with friends, or feel more confident in social settings. They may believe that drinking or smoking will make them more relaxed, fun, or attractive to others. In many social circles, substances become symbols of maturity or rebellion, and saying "no" can feel like saying "no" to belonging.

Many teenagers underestimate the risks or believe they are invincible to the dangers of substance abuse. They may not fully comprehend the potential for addiction, health problems, or the negative impact on their future. Often, the immediate reward of acceptance overshadows the long-term consequences.

Underlying Emotional Needs

At the heart of the need to fit in is often a deeper emotional struggle. Some teenagers lack confidence or struggle with feelings of insecurity, loneliness, or low self-worth. These feelings can make them more vulnerable to peer influence, as they seek affirmation and validation from others to fill the emotional gaps.

In some cases, substance abuse is not just about social pressure but also a coping mechanism. Teenagers facing stress, trauma, family problems, or mental health issues may turn to substances as a way to numb pain or escape reality temporarily.

Cultural and Environmental Factors

The environment teenagers grow up in plays a critical role. In communities where drug or alcohol use is normalized, glamorized, or easily accessible, the pressure to join in can be even stronger. Media portrayals of partying, rebellion, or substance use as a way to be popular further reinforce these behaviors.

Schools, neighborhoods, family dynamics, and socioeconomic status also influence how strongly the need to fit in pushes teens toward substance use. Teenagers in supportive, communicative families with clear boundaries may resist peer pressure better than those who feel neglected or misunderstood at home.

Breaking the Cycle: Building Healthy Belonging

Addressing the need to fit in without falling into substance abuse requires creating alternative spaces and communities where teenagers feel accepted and valued for who they truly are. Encouraging healthy friendships, extracurricular activities, mentorship programs, and open communication can help teens build a positive identity and confidence.

Parents, teachers, and community leaders can play a vital role by:

- *Modeling acceptance and understanding:*
  Teens need to feel loved and accepted unconditionally, which strengthens their inner security.

- *Teaching decision-making skills:*
  Empowering teens with tools to say no and make choices aligned with their values can build resilience.

- *Encouraging critical thinking:*
  Helping teens question media messages and peer group norms can reduce the blind following of risky behaviors.

- *Providing support for emotional needs:*
  Recognizing signs of stress, anxiety, or depression and offering counseling or support can reduce the reliance on substances.

The Importance of Identity Beyond the Peer Group

Helping teenagers develop a strong sense of self that is not dependent solely on peer acceptance is crucial. When teens understand their own worth, values, and purpose, they become less susceptible to the pressure to conform blindly. They can choose friendships and activities that nourish their growth instead of compromising it.

Teenagers who experience belonging in multiple positive areas; family, church, sports, arts, and community, have more options to find acceptance without resorting to unhealthy choices. This diversified sense of belonging acts as a buffer against peer pressure.

The need to fit in is a natural and powerful force in the world of teenagers today. While it can motivate positive social connections, it also exposes young people to the risk of substance abuse when acceptance is tied to unhealthy behaviors. Recognizing this dynamic is the first step toward supporting teenagers to navigate peer pressure wisely. By creating environments of acceptance, equipping teens with strong values, and addressing their emotional needs, we can help them find true belonging, one that enriches rather than endangers their lives.

8.2 Drugs, Alcohol, and Risky Behavior

Teenagers today face many challenges that can significantly affect their lives and futures. Among the most serious are drugs, alcohol, and risky behaviors. Understanding these issues is essential for parents, teachers, and teens themselves, so that they can make informed choices and avoid the many dangers involved.

The Role of Peer Pressure

At the heart of much substance use among teenagers is peer pressure. Teenagers are naturally influenced by the people around them: their friends, classmates, and social groups. This influence can sometimes push them to experiment with drugs or alcohol, even if they might not have done so on their own. The desire to fit in, be accepted, or avoid rejection is a powerful force during adolescence.

Many teens believe that using substances will make them seem more mature, cool, or "grown-up." They may also think it will help them escape stress, anxiety, or the pressures of school and family life. Yet these beliefs often lead to risky choices with serious consequences.

Common Substances and Their Effects

- **Alcohol** is the most commonly used substance among teenagers. Although often seen as socially acceptable, alcohol is a depressant that impairs judgment, coordination, and decision-making. Drinking alcohol at a young age can disrupt brain development and increase the risk of addiction later in life. Teens who drink are also more likely to engage in dangerous behaviors such as drunk driving, unprotected intimacies, or violence.

- **Drugs** vary widely in type and effect. Soft drugs are frequently used and often perceived as harmless or even medicinal. However, regular soft drug use can affect memory, learning, and motivation. Other drugs, such as hard drugs, are far more dangerous and highly addictive. These substances can cause severe physical and mental health problems, including overdose.

- **Prescription medications** are another area of concern. Many teenagers misuse prescription drugs, such as painkillers or stimulants, either by taking them without a prescription or using them in ways not intended by a doctor. This misuse can quickly lead to dependence or addiction and may expose teens to dangerous side effects.

Risky Behavior Linked to Substance Use

Substance use rarely occurs in isolation. It is often accompanied by risky behaviors that put teenagers in harm's way. These include:

- *Unsafe activity:* Teenagers under the influence of drugs or alcohol are less likely to make safe and informed choices, which can increase the chances of infections and unintended pregnancies."

- *Violence and aggression:* Intoxication can lower inhibitions and increase impulsiveness, sometimes leading to fights, assaults, or other violent acts.

The Cycle of Addiction and Despair

For some teenagers, experimentation turns into addiction, a powerful, often invisible force that controls their lives. Addiction is not simply a lack of willpower; it is a chronic disease that changes the brain and behavior. Teens struggling with addiction may feel trapped in a cycle of use and isolation.

This cycle can lead to mental health problems such as depression and anxiety. The connection between substance abuse and mental health is complex and requires compassionate, professional intervention.

Prevention and Support

Prevention is the best defense against the dangers of drugs, alcohol, and risky behavior. Families, schools, and communities all play vital roles in helping teenagers resist peer pressure and make healthy choices.

- *Open communication:* Teens need to feel safe talking about their fears, challenges, and experiences without fear of judgment or punishment. Parents and caregivers can build trust by listening actively and offering support.

- *Education:* Providing accurate, age-appropriate information about the effects and risks of substances helps teenagers understand the consequences before they experiment.

- *Healthy alternatives:* Encouraging participation in sports, arts, clubs, and other positive activities gives teens a sense of belonging and purpose without relying on substances.

- *Role models and mentors:* Positive adult role models who demonstrate healthy behavior can influence teens more than warnings or rules alone.

- *Professional help:* When substance use or risky behavior has become a problem, seeking help from counselors, therapists, or rehabilitation programs is crucial. Early intervention increases the chance of recovery.

Encouraging Resilience and Self-Worth

Ultimately, the best protection for teenagers against drugs, alcohol, and risky behavior is a strong sense of self-worth and resilience. Teens who believe in their value, purpose, and ability to overcome challenges are more likely to say no to harmful influences. Building these qualities requires consistent encouragement, love, and guidance from adults and peers alike.

8.3 Finding Real Friends

One of the greatest challenges teenagers face today is navigating peer pressure, especially when it comes to risky behaviors like substance abuse. But underlying this challenge is a deeper issue: the search for real, authentic friendships. Finding true friends is not just about having people to hang out with; it's about discovering those who support, encourage, and help us grow in positive ways.

Why Peer Pressure is So Powerful

Teenagers are at a stage of life where identity, belonging, and acceptance become central. The need to fit in with a group often outweighs individual judgment or values. This natural desire can lead to experimenting with things like alcohol, drugs, or other risky behaviors, especially when friends or acquaintances encourage it.

Peer pressure can be explicit, where someone directly offers or urges a teen to join in, or subtle, through unspoken expectations or a fear of being left out. The problem is not friendship itself, but the type of influence friends can have. Good friends build each other up; bad influences can lead to bad choices.

The Heart of Friendship: Trust and Respect

At the core of any real friendship is trust. When a friend truly cares about you, they respect your feelings, your boundaries, and your dreams. They do not pressure you to do things that make you uncomfortable or harm your future.

Real friends are those who stand with you when others criticize you, who listen when you're struggling, and who encourage you to be your best self, not just follow the crowd. They are honest with you, even when it's hard, because they want to see you succeed and be safe.

Recognizing True Friends

How can teenagers recognize real friends in a world full of superficial connections? Here are some signs of genuine friendship:

- *They listen without judgment.* Real friends give you space to share your thoughts and feelings without immediately trying to change or criticize you.

- *They encourage your good choices.* Instead of pushing you toward risky behavior, they celebrate your achievements and support your goals.

- *They respect your 'no'.* If you decline an invitation or say no to something, they don't guilt-trip you or bully you.

- *They stand up for you.* When others try to pressure or bully you, true friends defend and protect you.

- *They are reliable and consistent.* You can count on them all the time.

The Danger of "Fake" Friends

"Fake" friends often come with conditions, like only sticking around when it benefits them or when you do what they want. They may pressure you to drink, try drugs, or skip school just to "fit in" or look cool.

These relationships drain energy and self-esteem and can lead to dangerous paths. The desire to be accepted can make it hard to walk away from fake friends, but doing so is often necessary for personal safety and growth.

How to Find Real Friends

Finding real friends requires courage and intentionality. Here are some practical ways teenagers can build authentic friendships:

- *Know yourself first.* When you understand your own values, interests, and limits, it becomes easier to attract friends who share and respect them.

- *Join positive groups or clubs.* Activities like sports, art, music, or volunteering bring together people with shared passions and positive mindsets.

- *Be a good friend yourself.* Treat others with kindness, honesty, and respect. Genuine friendships often start with one person taking the first step.

- *Set boundaries.* It's fine to say no to things that make you uncomfortable, even if it means risking rejection from some peers. Real friends will respect your boundaries.

- *Look beyond popularity.* Sometimes, the most loyal friends aren't the ones with the biggest social circle or loudest voice, but those who quietly support and accept you.

- *Be patient.* Deep friendships take time to develop. Don't rush into relationships just to avoid loneliness.

Overcoming Loneliness and the Fear of Rejection

Many teenagers succumb to peer pressure because they fear being alone or rejected. But loneliness can be a season that leads to growth. Being alone with your thoughts allows you to build confidence and clarify what you really want in friends and life.

Remember, it's better to have a few true friends than many fake ones. Quality over quantity is key.

The Role of Family and Mentors

While peers play a big role during the teenage years, family and trusted adults remain vital sources of support. Parents, older siblings, teachers, coaches, and mentors can offer guidance, listen to your concerns, and help you develop healthy relationships.

Teens should be encouraged to seek advice from these trusted individuals when they feel pressured or uncertain about friendships. Sometimes, just talking about struggles can make a big difference.

Real Friendship Helps Resist Substance Abuse

When teenagers find real friends who care about their well-being, it becomes easier to resist peer pressure related to substance use. Good friends offer alternatives for fun and help each other stay accountable.

For example, instead of going to a party where drinking is expected, real friends might plan a movie night, sports event, or other activities that don't involve substances.

Real friendships build a foundation for healthier decisions, stronger self-esteem, and a future full of promise.

Chapter 9

Identity and Belonging

9.1 Navigating Identity

Teenagers today are growing up in a world that talks more openly about identity, gender, and sexuality than any generation before them. With the rise of social media, global conversations, and shifting cultural norms, young people are exposed to a wide variety of views; some grounded in truth, others in confusion. While this offers opportunities for learning, it also creates pressure and uncertainty for many teenagers.

The teenage years are already a time of change and questioning. Physically, emotionally, and socially, teens are transitioning from childhood to adulthood. During this time, questions like "Who am I?" and "Where do I fit in?" become more intense. Add to that today's loud and complex conversations around gender and sexuality, and many teens are left feeling overwhelmed, isolated, or pressured to adopt labels.

Understanding the World Teens Live In

It's important to acknowledge that many teens are not actively seeking to rebel; they are searching for truth, safety, and acceptance. They are bombarded with messages from celebrities, influencers, online communities, and sometimes even schools that tell them gender is fluid, sexuality is a spectrum, and personal feelings define reality. Some teens may begin questioning their gender identity or sexual orientation simply because it's popular to explore these topics in their social circles.

This questioning is often about curiosity, peer pressure, or the fear of being left out. Teenagers want to be seen, loved, and included. In many places today, identifying as lgbtq+ is celebrated, while standing for biblical truth is criticized or labeled as hatred. As a result, Christian teens especially, may feel caught between loyalty to God and the desire to belong in their peer group.

What Does the Bible Say?

The Bible provides clarity in the midst of confusion. ***Genesis 1:27 tells us that God created humans in His image: "male and female He created them."*** This means that our gender is not just a social construct; it is a part of God's design. Our identity is not something we must invent; it is something we receive from our Creator. Our value comes from being made by God, not from how we feel or what others say.

Guiding Teenagers with Grace and Truth

Adults, parents, and church leaders must learn to speak to teens with both *grace and truth*. Shouting at teenagers or ignoring their questions does not help them. Instead, we need to listen to them with compassion, create safe spaces for discussion, and teach them to root their identity in Christ.

Young people need to hear that their feelings do not define them; God does. They may feel confused, but feelings come and go. God's truth is steady and reliable. Helping them grow in their relationship with Jesus Christ is the best way to anchor them in truth while the world around them shifts.

Churches can support teenagers by:

- Teaching clearly what the Bible says about identity, gender, and sexuality.

- Providing mentorship and discipleship for teens struggling with these issues.

- Encouraging open conversations without fear.

- Training youth leaders to respond with wisdom, compassion, and biblical knowledge.

Parents can also play a crucial role by:

- Building a strong relationship with their teenager based on trust and love.

- Asking questions without judgment and listening carefully.

- Praying daily for their teen's heart and mind to be guarded by God's truth.

- Modeling confidence in their own identity in Christ.

Belonging in the Family of God

Every teenager longs to belong to a family, to a friend group, to something meaningful. The Church must be a place where teenagers find their deepest sense of belonging. When they know they are accepted, valued, and loved, not for what they say or do, but simply because God made them, they begin to build their identity on solid ground.

Let us remind them: "You are not defined by your gender, your attractions, or what others say about you. You are defined by God, who calls you His child." In Christ, we all find our truest identity; not just teenagers, but every one of us. The journey may be full of questions, but the destination is clear: we are called to be conformed to the image of Christ, walking in truth and love.

9.2 Faith, Values, and Peer Influence

Teenage years are full of changes; not only physical and emotional, but also spiritual and social. In the heart of every teenager is a search for meaning, direction, and belonging. Faith and personal values can provide a strong foundation in this period. However, the voices of peers, the lure of trends, and the fear of being different often challenge this foundation.

The Power of Faith

Faith gives teenagers a sense of identity and purpose. For those raised in Christian homes, faith often begins as something inherited or taught in Sunday school or during family prayers. But adolescence is the time when this faith must become personal. It's no longer just what mom and dad believe. Teenagers begin to ask, *"Do I really believe in God?" "Is this faith real for me?" "How does God fit into my daily activities?" But that should not be the question normally. The question is, how do I fit into God's plan for me?*

A teenager who discovers a living relationship with Jesus finds an anchor for life. Faith answers deep questions like *"Who am I?"* and *"Why am I here?"* It provides assurance in a world full of contradictions. In a time where social media creates pressure to be popular, look perfect, or follow every trend, faith in Christ reminds teens that they are loved unconditionally and created with purpose.

Building Values That Last

Values are the principles we live by: honesty, respect, responsibility, purity, love, compassion, and more. Many teenagers struggle with what values to adopt because they see conflicting messages everywhere.

One moment, they hear about forgiveness at church; the next, they see revenge glorified in music or movies. One moment, they learn about sexual purity in youth group; the next, their friends make fun of virginity.

That is why Christian values must be rooted deeply in truth, not in emotions or popularity. God's Word becomes the measuring stick. When a teenager learns to read the Bible regularly and receives discipleship, he begins to internalize values that are not only right but life-giving.

For example, the value of integrity. A teenager who chooses to be honest even when it's hard develops character. Or a young girl who chooses modesty and respect for her body because she sees herself as a temple of God grows in confidence. Values give direction, and when they are based on faith, they have eternal significance.

Peer Influence: The Hidden Force

Peers play a huge role in shaping a teenager's life. Friends influence what teens wear, how they talk, what music they like, and how they feel about themselves. Peer pressure can be positive or negative, but it is always powerful. Many teens end up compromising their faith or values, not because they don't believe in them, but because they fear rejection from their peers.

A boy who prays at home may pretend he doesn't believe in God at school because his friends laugh at religion. A girl who's committed to purity may find herself slowly giving in because all her friends talk about dating, and she doesn't want to be the odd one out.

That is why teens need to be surrounded by a faith-based community, such as a strong church youth group, Christian mentors, or even just one or two solid Christian friends. The Bible says, *"Bad company corrupts good character" (1 Corinthians 15:33),* but it also shows how good company can build faith. Just look at the friendship of Daniel, Shadrach, Meshach, and Abednego in Babylon. They stood together, even when the culture around them pressured them to bow.

When Faith and Friends Collide

What happens when a teenager's faith contradicts what their friends believe or do? This is where the real test of conviction comes in. Choosing faith over friendship is never easy, but it is necessary. A wise teenager learns to say "no" with courage and "yes" with discernment.

Parents and youth leaders should help teenagers prepare for these situations by teaching them to respond with both boldness and grace. Not every peer who disagrees is an enemy. Sometimes, a firm but loving stand for righteousness can lead others to respect or even follow Christ.

Also, teens should learn to pray for their friends. Evangelism isn't only for adults; teenagers are powerful witnesses. When a teen lives out their faith authentically, without judgment but with joy and consistency, their peers notice. Over time, that influence can become **stronger** than peer pressure.

The Role of the Church and Family

The Church and the family must partner to help teenagers grow in their faith and values. Church should not just be a place of Sunday meetings, but a community that walks with teens through their real-life challenges. Parents must model the values they expect from their children. It's not enough to say "don't lie"; they must live honestly themselves. When teens see hypocrisy at home, they struggle to take faith seriously.

Discipleship programs, youth camps, mentorship, and regular discussions about life and values help teenagers feel heard and guided. Teens need a space where they can ask hard questions without fear, where doubts can be expressed, and where spiritual growth is encouraged, not forced.

In the world of teenagers today, faith in God, values, and peer influence form a triangle that can either build or break their sense of self. With the right support and intentional teaching, teenagers can learn to stand strong in their beliefs, make wise choices, and influence their world rather than being influenced by it. The Church must rise to walk beside them, not ahead of them. And we must remind them daily: *you are not alone, you are loved, and you are to shine.*

9.3 Where Do I Belong?

One of the deepest questions every teenager asks consciously or unconsciously is this: ***"Where do I belong?"*** Belonging is not just about being in a group or having a circle of friends. It's about feeling accepted, valued, and understood. For many teens, finding a sense of belonging is one of the most challenging parts of growing up, especially in today's world, where identity and social pressures are more complex than ever.

The teenage years are a season of discovery. You're no longer a child, but you're not yet a fully grown adult. You're figuring out who you are, what you believe, and how you fit into this big, complex world. As you do this, your heart naturally longs for a place or a group of people where you feel safe, seen, and supported.

The Search for Belonging

Teenagers today live in a world full of voices telling them where they *should* belong. Social media, school environments, TV shows, music, and even peer groups often shape how teens see themselves and where they believe they can fit in. Some feel they must change their appearance, interests, or even beliefs to be accepted. Others may feel excluded because of their background, identity, or cultural differences.

This longing for belonging can sometimes push teenagers into the wrong circles. When someone doesn't feel accepted at home, at church, or in school, they may turn to people who offer them attention, even if that group leads them down a harmful path. Gang involvement, harmful sexual relationships, addiction, and identity confusion often start with someone looking for love and belonging in the wrong places.

This shows just how powerful and essential the need to belong truly is.

God Created us to Belong

The good news is that you were **created to belong**, first and foremost, to **God**.

In Genesis, we see that God made us in His image, not to walk alone, but in relationship with Him and with others. Psalm 68:6 says, *"God sets the lonely in families."* That means God cares about your longing for connection. He didn't create you to wander through life feeling like you don't fit anywhere. He wants you to find your identity in Him and become part of His spiritual family.

Belonging in Christ is different from worldly belonging. In the world, you may be accepted based on how you look, what you wear, or how popular you are. In Christ, you are accepted because of who He is, not because of what you do. When you know that you are loved by God, your sense of identity becomes rooted in something unshakable.

Ephesians 2:19 says, *"You are no longer foreigners and strangers, but fellow citizens with God's people and also members of His household."* That's powerful. No matter your past, your mistakes, or your questions, Jesus makes room for you in His family.

A Place in the Church

The local church should be one of the safest places for teenagers to find real belonging. Not a place of judgment or pressure, but a place of welcome and grace.

As a teenager, don't give up on the Church just because you don't see your perfect fit right away. Get involved. Join a Bible study. Talk to a youth leader. Ask questions. Share your heart. The more you open up, the more you will see that you're not the only one asking, "Where do I belong?" Many others are looking for the same thing, and God wants to build a beautiful community out of all your stories.

Navigating Questions About Identity

Belonging is closely tied to identity. Today, many teens wrestle with big questions about who they really are. These are not easy topics, and they often carry deep emotional weight.

It's alright to ask questions. But in the midst of the questions, keep your heart open to God's truth. Psalm 139:13-14 says, *"For You created my inmost being; You knit me together in my mother's womb. I praise You because I am fearfully and wonderfully made."*

You were made on purpose, with purpose. God doesn't make mistakes. Your value does not depend on how you feel in a moment or what others say about you. You are already loved and wanted by your Creator.

Finding Belonging Through Purpose

One of the best ways to discover where you belong is to start walking in your God-given purpose. Ask yourself: What do I love to do? What makes me come alive? What are the gifts God has placed inside of me?

When you start using your talents to serve others, whether through music, writing, helping younger kids, or praying for your friends, you'll begin to attract the right kind of people around you. Purpose draws community. When you're walking in your God-given calling, you will find people with similar hearts, and together you will experience true belonging.

The question "Where do I belong?" is not just a teenage question. It's a human one. But as a teenager, you have a special opportunity to find your true place; not just in the world, but in God's family, in His truth, and in His purpose for your life. You don't have to change who you are to be accepted. God welcomes you as you are, and He will lead you to the right people, the right mentors, and the right path in time.

9.4 Navigating Puberty

Puberty is one of life's greatest transitions; a bridge that carries a person from childhood into young adulthood. It's a season of stretching, discovery, and growth, not just physically, but emotionally, mentally, and spiritually. Understanding puberty can help you walk through it with confidence and peace, rather than fear or confusion.

Whether you're in the early stages or already noticing changes, it's important to know: *you are not alone*. Every adult you admire has gone through this stage, and so have millions of other young people across the world. Let's walk through it together.

When Does Puberty Start?

Puberty usually begins between the ages of *8 and 13* for girls and between *9 and 14* for boys, but everyone develops at their own pace. Some people start earlier, others later, and that's completely normal. Your body follows the timeline that God has uniquely designed for you. So, if your friends seem to be changing faster or slower than you, don't worry. Puberty is not a race. What matters most is growing with patience, understanding, and confidence that you are becoming exactly who you're meant to be, right on time.

A Time of Growth: Inside and Out

One of the most remarkable things about puberty is how quickly things start to shift. Your voice might sound different to you, your thoughts might deepen, and your relationships might evolve. But while these changes are very real, the most important transformations aren't always visible.

You might begin to see the world around you in new ways. Your ability to think critically increases. You may start asking deep questions about your purpose, future, or even about God. That is because your mind is maturing. It's a beautiful sign that you are growing!

With growth, however, comes a certain amount of discomfort. That's natural. Change, even good change, can be challenging. Puberty brings moments of uncertainty, but also moments of self-discovery. It is during this time that many teens begin to discover their gifts, passions, and calling.

Emotional Changes and Mood Swings

One day you might feel joyful and on top of the world, and the next day you might feel overwhelmed, irritated, or discouraged. That's not because you're "being difficult"; it's often the result of your emotions adjusting as your hormones shift.

Think of emotions during puberty as waves. Some are small and easy to ride. Others might crash into you unexpectedly. But like every wave, they will rise and fall. Learning how to *recognize, manage,* and *express* your emotions is one of the most important skills you can develop during this season.

Here are a few tips to help:

- *Pause and breathe* before reacting. Don't let feelings control your actions.

- *Talk it out.* Share how you're feeling with a trusted adult, friend, or mentor.

- *Use writing or art* to express what's inside.

- **Pray.** God knows how you feel even before you say it. Talking to Him brings peace.

This emotional journey is part of your preparation for maturity. As you learn to handle your emotions with wisdom, you are laying a strong foundation for your future.

Friendships and Social Circles

Puberty doesn't just change your body and emotions; it can also affect your friendships and how you relate to others. You might find yourself drifting away from old friends and becoming closer to new ones. You may even start to care more about how others see you.

That's completely normal.

You may also become more aware of group dynamics; who's popular, who's left out, or how you fit in. It's easy to get caught up in trying to impress others or to compare yourself to people around you. But remember this:

*Your worth is not found in people's opinions; **it is found in God's love for you.***

Use this season to choose friends who:

- Encourage you to do what's right

- Speak kindly and respectfully

- Bring out the best in you

- Respect your boundaries and values.

Friendships during puberty may change, but that's alright. Stay open to new connections, but also guard your heart. And if you feel lonely, know that this is just a season. You will find your people who understand you, celebrate you, and walk with you in truth.

"*Let no one despise your youth, but be an example to the believers in word, in conduct, in love, in spirit, in faith, in purity.*" 1 Timothy 4:12

Building Healthy Habits

One of the best things you can do during puberty is to build healthy routines. As you grow, your body and mind require new forms of care and discipline.

Here are some key areas to focus on:

1. **Sleep and Rest**
   Your body is doing a lot of work behind the scenes. Getting enough rest is vital. Most teens need about 8 to 10 hours of sleep per night. Without enough rest, you may feel irritated, sluggish, or have trouble focusing.

2. **Nutrition and Water**
   What you eat now can set the tone for your energy, focus, and overall health. Aim for a balance: fruits, vegetables, proteins, grains, and plenty of water. Try not to skip meals and avoid too much sugar or processed food.

3. **Movement and Exercise**
   Staying active helps not only your body but also your mind. Walking, biking, dancing, or playing sports can improve your mood, help you sleep better, and make you feel stronger.

4. **Personal Hygiene**

With the changes in your body, it becomes even more important to stay clean and fresh. Take regular showers, brush your teeth, wear clean clothes, and take care of your skin and hair.

These small habits might seem boring, but they add up to big results. They help you feel confident, stay healthy, and show others that you respect yourself and your surroundings.

Becoming Spiritually Aware

As you grow physically and emotionally, your spirit is also maturing. Many teens begin to ask questions about God, faith, life's purpose, and right and wrong during puberty. That is a beautiful thing.

Puberty is not just a time of physical transition; it is also a time when God starts drawing you closer to Him in new ways. You may begin to hear His voice more clearly, feel His presence more personally, and respond to Him more deeply.

Here's how you can grow spiritually during this time:

- *Make time for prayer and Bible reading,* even if it's just 5–10 minutes a day.

- *Ask questions about faith* and seek answers from your pastor, parents, or youth leaders.

- *Get involved in your Church,* youth groups, or Christian clubs.

- *Write down what God is teaching you* or showing you in a journal.

Never think you're too young to be used by God. Many powerful men and women of faith started hearing God's call as teenagers. This is your season to begin your walk with Him in a deeper way.

You Are Becoming

Puberty is a process of *becoming*. You're not the child you used to be, but you're also not yet the adult you will become. It's like being in the middle of a journey. And that's exactly where God wants to meet you.

So don't rush it.

Don't compare your growth to others. Don't fear the changes or feel ashamed of them. You are being shaped into a young adult: someone full of potential, wisdom, creativity, strength, and purpose.

Surround yourself with people who care. Make good choices, even when no one's watching. Keep learning. Stay true to who you are. And most of all, stay close to God.

You may not always understand everything, but you can trust that God sees you, loves you, and is guiding you every step of the way.

This verse reminds you that even during this season of change, you can shine as an example of faith, love, and strength. God is with you in your growth.

A Prayer for the Journey Through Puberty

Dear Heavenly Father,

Thank You for the way You created me; with purpose, beauty, and care. Even when I feel uncertain or uncomfortable, help me to remember that You are guiding me through this season of change. Teach me how to grow with wisdom, patience, and confidence. Strengthen my mind, my heart, and my body.

Surround me with good friends, loving family, and wise mentors who can help me walk this journey with joy. When I feel confused, remind me of Your peace. When I feel weak, remind me of Your strength. And when I feel alone, remind me that You are always near.

Help me to grow not just physically, but also in my faith and character. Shape me into the person You have designed me to be. Use this time to draw me closer to You.

In Jesus' name,
Amen.

PART 3

HOW WE CAN HELP

Chapter 10

How Parents Can Connect, Not Control

10.1 Building Trust

One of the greatest challenges parents face in today's fast-changing world is learning how to connect with their teenagers without controlling them. As children become teens, they begin to develop a strong sense of independence and identity. This transformation can be confusing not only for the teen but also for parents. Yet, this is not a time for fear or withdrawal; it is a season that requires *trust*. And trust is not built overnight; it is cultivated through intentional choices, daily consistency, and grace.

Trust Begins with Respect

Respect is the foundation of any healthy relationship, including that between parents and teenagers. Teenagers long to be heard, valued, and taken seriously. When parents interrupt, dismiss, or belittle their opinions, it sends a message that their voice doesn't matter. Over time, this breaks down trust and invites rebellion or emotional withdrawal.

Instead of assuming that authority must always mean command and control, wise parents learn to *listen first*. Ask your teens their opinion on matters, even small ones. "What do you think about this?" or "How would you handle this situation?" may seem like simple questions, but they help communicate that you see your teen as a thinking individual, not just a child.

Trust is built when a parent respects the process of maturity. That means recognizing that mistakes might happen, and not everyone needs to be punished. Some mistakes are simply part of growing up and learning. When parents correct with kindness and give space to learn, teens feel safe. They begin to open up more because they know they won't be judged or shut down.

Creating a Safe Environment

Teenagers today face pressures unlike any previous generation. Social media, peer comparison, academic stress, and questions about identity bombard them daily. In such a world, home should be their safest place, and parents should be their strongest allies.

To build trust, parents must create an emotionally safe environment. Avoid sarcasm and harsh criticism. Instead, affirm your teens regularly. Celebrate their strengths and express gratitude when they show honesty, even if what they share is difficult to understand. For instance, if your teen admits to struggling with temptation, don't explode or immediately lecture. First, acknowledge the courage it took to be honest. This response deepens trust and encourages future transparency.

Parents must also model emotional honesty. If you make a mistake, apologize. If you are struggling emotionally, share within limits. When teens see that their parents are real people who also deal with challenges and are growing, they feel less isolated in their journey, and that creates a connection.

Communicate Expectations with Grace

While connection is crucial, it doesn't mean abandoning boundaries. Teenagers need structure, but they also need understanding. The difference between control and connection lies in how expectations are communicated.

Controlling parents often use fear and manipulation: "If you don't do this, I will…" Connected parents, on the other hand, use guidance and shared responsibility. They explain the *why* behind a rule and invite discussion. For example, rather than saying, "You're not allowed to go to that party because I said so," you might say, "I'm concerned about the safety of that party and the influence of the crowd. Can we talk about it together?"

When teens feel included in decision-making, they are more likely to own the boundaries themselves. Connection-based parenting teaches responsibility through trust rather than compliance through fear.

Keep the Door Open

No matter how mature teens become, they will still need their parents, just in a different way. They may not always want hugs or bedtime stories, but they do need conversations, encouragement, presence, and support.

Even if your teens are going through a season where they pull away, resist the urge to chase or control. Instead, keep the door open. That means saying things like:

- "I'm here whenever you want to talk."

- "I may not understand everything, but I care deeply and I'm willing to listen and pray about it."

- "No matter what, I will never stop loving you."

Sometimes, trust is built in quiet consistency. Being present in the background, showing up at their games, respecting their privacy, and maintaining family traditions, even when they roll their eyes, all that speaks volumes over time.

Pray and Trust God

Finally, building trust with your teenager means trusting God. No parent can be perfect. Even the best efforts may not produce immediate results. But when you entrust your teen to God's hands, you acknowledge that He is the ultimate Shepherd of their heart.

Pray for wisdom daily. Pray for patience. Pray that your teen's heart would stay tender toward truth. And when you make a mistake, trust God to fill in the gaps.

Remember, God cares about your teens even more than you do. Your role is to reflect His grace and truth, not to replace Him. Connecting with your teen, rather than controlling them, aligns your parenting with God's heart. You become not just a parent, but a trusted guide on their journey to adulthood.

10.2 Listening More Than Speaking

One of the deepest longings of today's teenagers is simply to be heard. In a world full of noise, from social media, peer pressure, school expectations, and their own swirling emotions, what they crave at home is a safe space where they can speak freely without fear of judgment, correction, or interruption. That safe space begins with a parent who chooses to listen more than speak.

Too often, well-meaning parents rush to advise, correct, or even lecture their teens at the first sign of a problem. While the intention may be to help, the effect is often the opposite. The teenager shuts down, becomes defensive, or simply tunes out. Why? Because the message they receive is: *"You're not really interested in understanding me; you just want to fix me."*

But teenagers don't always want a solution; they want a connection. They want to be understood, validated, and taken seriously. When parents develop the habit of listening, truly listening, they create a bridge of trust that opens the heart of their child.

What Listening Looks Like

Listening is not just the act of being quiet while the teen talks. It is active. It involves paying attention to both words and emotions, maintaining eye contact, and showing genuine interest. It's about noticing the things your child says *and* the things they struggle to say.

This means putting down the phone, turning off the TV, and giving them your full attention when they speak. It means not interrupting, correcting, or jumping in with a "better version" of their story. It means asking open-ended questions like, "How did that make you feel?" or "What do you think you'll do about it?" instead of leading with statements like, "Here's what I would have done."

Listening is an act of humility. It says, *"I don't have all the answers, but I care deeply about your heart."*

Why Listening Builds Respect

Teenagers are in the process of forming their identity. As they try to discover who they are, they test boundaries, express strong opinions, and sometimes rebel. When parents choose to listen instead of dominating the conversation, they communicate something powerful: *"Your thoughts matter. Your voice matters. You matter."*

This builds mutual respect. Teenagers are more likely to listen to parents who have consistently listened to them. They become more open to advice when it comes from someone who first made the effort to understand them.

Respect is not demanded; it is earned. And one of the quickest paths to earning it is by practicing the art of listening.

Shifting from Control to Connection

Controlling parents focus on managing every detail of their teenager's life: grades, friends, activities, appearance, and choices. While some structure is necessary, too much control suffocates growth. It prevents teens from learning how to think, decide, and take responsibility.

Connection, on the other hand, brings maturity. It's built through honest conversations, shared experiences, and moments of vulnerability. And all begins with listening.

Parents don't need to solve every problem or give an answer for every issue. Sometimes, the greatest help is simply being present and saying, "I hear you." Teenagers grow stronger when they feel supported, not when they feel micromanaged.

Jesus and Listening

Even in Scripture, we see the power of listening. Jesus, though all-knowing, often asked questions. He listened to people's hearts before responding. With the woman at the well (John 4), He listened deeply to her story and pain. With the disciples, He allowed them to speak their doubts and fears. He modeled a way of relating that invited trust.

As parents, we can follow His example. Before speaking, we can pause, ask, and listen. When we do, we give our teenagers a glimpse of God's patience, compassion, and love.

A Listening Challenge for Parents

Try this: for one week, commit to listening at least twice as much as you speak when interacting with your teens. Resist the urge to immediately correct or guide. Ask more questions. Reflect back what you hear. Watch how your teenager's openness begins to shift.

Listening doesn't mean we agree with everything they say. It means we value them enough to hear them out. And in a noisy world, that kind of listening is a priceless gift.

10.3 Boundaries with Love

Raising teenagers in today's fast-moving, emotionally complex world is a sacred trust and a daily challenge. Many parents struggle to strike the right balance between guidance and freedom. Some lean too heavily on control, while others, out of fear of losing connection, neglect discipline altogether. But biblical wisdom and modern research agree that boundaries set in love create the safest and most empowering environment for teenagers.

Love is Not the Absence of Boundaries

One of the most misunderstood ideas in modern parenting is that love should feel like freedom without limits. But real love, God's kind of love, always includes discipline. Hebrews 12:6 reminds us, *"For whom the Lord loves He chastens..."* This doesn't mean harshness or punishment, but a loving correction that protects, directs, and empowers.

Boundaries are not walls; they are fences with gates. They are not meant to lock teenagers in but to guide them toward maturity, responsibility, and self-control. When boundaries are set in anger or fear, they feel like chains. But when they are given in love, with explanation, consistency, and respect, they become lifelines. They teach teenagers how to make wise decisions, even when their parents are not around.

What Loving Boundaries Look Like

Loving boundaries are clear, consistent, and reasonable. They are communicated in advance, not screamed in moments of frustration. For example, if a parent sets a curfew, it should be based on age, safety, and mutual understanding. It shouldn't be a sudden rule shouted on the night of a social event. Instead, a loving parent might say: "We trust you and want you to enjoy time with your friends. But part of our responsibility is knowing you're safe. That's why we ask you to be home by 10 PM on school nights."

The teenager may still push back. That's normal. But when the boundary is communicated with calm, care, and consistency, over time, it is respected.

Here are a few examples of healthy, loving boundaries:

- *Technology Time:* "Phones and devices are placed in the family charging station by 9 PM. Not as punishment, but to protect sleep and mental health."

- *Respectful Communication:* "In this home, we don't yell or insult each other. You can be angry, but you must express it respectfully."

- *Academic Responsibility:* "We expect you to do your homework before entertainment. If grades slip, privileges like video games will pause until improvement is seen."

- *Friendship and Influence:* "We want to know your friends. You can spend time with them, but not with those who constantly encourage bad behavior."

Every family will have slightly different boundaries, but the principle remains: love sets limits that protect and prepare teenagers for real adult life.

The Heart Behind the Boundary

Teenagers are very perceptive. They don't just hear *what* we say, they sense *why* we say it. If they feel that rules are rooted in fear, control, or distrust, they will resist. But if they see that boundaries are rooted in love, care, and wisdom, they are more likely to cooperate, even if they don't like it in the moment.

Jesus Christ is our model. He never forced people to follow Him, yet He clearly laid out the cost and the way of life that brings true freedom. He said, *"If you love Me, keep My commandments"* (John 14:15). These are loving boundaries; not forced obedience but willing trust built on love.

When parents approach boundaries from a relational heart instead of a controlling spirit, they create a home where trust grows. It's fine to say, "I'm setting this boundary because I love you too much to let you harm yourself," or "This is not about control; it's about helping you become the best version of yourself."

Respecting the Growing Independence

As children grow into teenagers, their need for autonomy increases. This is not rebellion; it's part of development. The mistake many parents make is clinging tightly just when their teens need room to stretch their wings. Instead of pulling the rope tighter, parents should gradually *lengthen* the rope, *but keep it tied.*

For example, allow more say in clothing choices, music, or scheduling, within agreed boundaries. Say things like: "I want you to make your own choices, but let's talk about the possible consequences together first."

Remember, boundaries don't stop independence; they support *healthy* independence. They say, "We believe in you enough to give you space, but we love you enough to still walk beside you."

When Boundaries Are Broken

It's inevitable: boundaries will be tested. That's part of being a teenager. The goal of boundaries isn't perfection, it's growth. When a teenager breaks a boundary, parents should respond with grace *and* consequences.

Consequences should be logical and connected. For instance, if they misuse their phone, take it away for a time, not out of anger, but to protect and guide. And always, always follow correction with affirmation. "I understand that this happened, but I still love you. I believe in you. Let's learn from this and move forward."

Pray and Stay Consistent

No parent can do this perfectly. But with prayer, patience, and support, it's possible to set boundaries that lead to deep trust and connection. Ask the Holy Spirit daily for wisdom. Ask your teenager for feedback sometimes. Stay humble and teachable.

When boundaries are set with love, enforced with grace, and explained with understanding, they become a bridge, not a barrier. They don't drive teenagers away; they lead them home to responsibility, maturity, and relationship.

Chapter 11

The Role of Teachers and Mentors

11.1 Teaching with Empathy

Teachers and mentors are not just educators or supervisors; they are shapers of destiny. But to reach the heart of a teenager, empathy must be the starting point.

Empathy is not simply feeling sorry for someone; it is stepping into their shoes, listening without judgment, and responding with kindness and understanding. When a teacher teaches with empathy, they see more than just a struggling student or a rebellious teen, they see a soul in transition, a life full of potential, and someone worth investing in.

Let's consider the classroom. A teenager walks in with a sullen expression, avoids eye contact, and seems disengaged. A teacher who lacks empathy might immediately label that student as lazy or disrespectful. But a teacher with empathy pauses to ask, "What's really going on here?"

Maybe that teenager didn't sleep the night before because of tension at home. Maybe they haven't eaten breakfast. Maybe they're battling anxiety or silently hurting about something they can't talk about.

Empathetic teaching takes time, patience, and prayer. It means sometimes laying aside the lesson plan to have a real conversation. It means understanding that the goal of education is not just the transmission of facts, but the *transformation of lives*.

Empathy in teaching also requires active listening. Teenagers often speak more with their actions than their words. A teacher who listens between the lines will recognize when a joke is really a cry for help, or when silence is masking a storm within. When students know they are seen, heard, and valued, their hearts begin to open, and then true learning can begin.

Jesus Christ, the Master Teacher, modeled this perfectly. He didn't just teach sermons; He sat with people, asked questions, and looked into their hearts. He saw the Samaritan woman's thirst for love, Zacchaeus's longing for acceptance, and the rich young ruler's struggle with identity. When we teach teenagers today with the same spirit of compassion and grace, we become Christ's hands extended to them.

Teenagers are at a fragile stage of self-discovery. Empathetic teachers can help them navigate that journey by creating a safe, respectful environment in the classroom. Instead of humiliating a student for a test, an empathetic teacher might say, "Let's go through this together. I know you're capable. Let me help you figure out where you're struggling." That kind of support builds not just academic strength, but emotional resilience.

Empathy also applies to *discipline*. A mentor or teacher may need to correct a teenager, but how it is done makes all the difference. Harsh, cold rebukes often harden the heart. But discipline wrapped in love and concern, such as saying, "I care about your future, and that's why I'm addressing this," can help the student grow. Teenagers respond better when they feel respected, not belittled.

Let's not forget that teachers and mentors are often the only stable adult presence in some teens' lives. Your smile, your words of encouragement, and your belief in their potential may be the lifeline that keeps them going. One positive, empathetic relationship can outweigh ten negative ones.

Finally, teaching with empathy is not just about helping teenagers; it also transforms the teacher. As you connect with the dreams, and struggles of young people, your heart will be stretched. You will grow in patience, wisdom, and love. And you will find joy in watching the seed you planted bloom into a beautiful life.

Empathetic teaching is Kingdom work. It's more than a job, it's a calling. And in a world where so many teenagers feel unseen and misunderstood, an empathetic teacher or mentor becomes the bridge between confusion and clarity, between despair and hope, between drifting and destiny.

Let us rise to that calling.

11.2 Becoming a Safe Adult

In the complex and often turbulent world that teenagers navigate today, the presence of safe, trustworthy adults can make an enormous difference. Teachers and mentors who consciously choose to become "safe adults" offer young people a refuge, a place where they can be heard, understood, and supported without fear of judgment or rejection. But what does it truly mean to be a safe adult? And how can those who work closely with teenagers step into this vital role?

Understanding the Need for Safe Adults

Teenagers today face unprecedented pressures: social media scrutiny, academic stress, identity confusion, peer pressure, and in many cases, family instability or trauma. These challenges make it difficult for many young people to find someone to trust fully. While parents often play a central role in a child's life, teachers and mentors frequently become the "other adults" teenagers turn to when they need guidance, reassurance, or simply someone to listen.

Safe adults serve as anchors in this chaotic landscape. They provide emotional safety and consistent support that teenagers need to develop resilience and confidence. When a young person senses they are accepted and valued without conditions, it gives a sense of belonging, a fundamental human need that is often unmet in adolescence.

Characteristics of a Safe Adult

- *Approachability*
  Safe adults are approachable and open. They create an environment where teenagers feel comfortable sharing their thoughts and struggles. This does not mean that they must be best friends with every young person, but rather that their demeanor communicates: "You can come to me without fear." Simple gestures like maintaining eye contact, listening attentively, and showing genuine interest build bridges of trust.

- *Consistency and Reliability*
  Teenagers, more than anyone, notice inconsistency. Safe adults show up when they say they will, keep confidence, and follow through on promises. This reliability sends the message that the young person matters, reinforcing their self-worth. It also creates a dependable framework within which teenagers can test out ideas, ask questions, and make mistakes without fear of abandonment.

- *Non-Judgmental Attitude*
  Adolescence is a time of experimentation and self-discovery, often accompanied by mistakes and rebellion. Safe adults maintain a non-judgmental stance, avoiding harsh criticism or dismissiveness. Instead, they seek to understand the teenager's perspective and offer guidance rooted in empathy. This approach opens doors for honest conversations and mutual respect.

- *Boundaries and Safety*
  While being approachable and empathetic, safe adults also establish clear boundaries. These boundaries are essential to create a secure space where teenagers know what is acceptable and what isn't. It's a balance between warmth and structure; too rigid, and teenagers may feel constrained; too lax, and they may feel unsafe or confused. Boundaries protect both the adult and the teenager and set a healthy example for respect and responsibility.

- *Empowerment over Control*
  Safe adults empower teenagers rather than control them. They encourage young people to think critically, make their own decisions, and develop autonomy. Rather than dictating what must be done, they guide by asking thoughtful questions and helping teenagers explore consequences. This empowers teens to own their choices and build confidence in their ability to navigate life.

Practical Steps to Becoming a Safe Adult

Teachers and mentors often ask, "How can I become more of a safe adult in the life of a teenager?" While this is a lifelong journey, some practical steps can help start the process:

- *Listen Actively:* When a teenager talks, listen without interrupting. Show through body language and responses that you value their voice.

- *Be Available:* Create times and spaces where teenagers know you are approachable, be it a weekly check-in, an open-door policy, or informal chats during breaks.

- *Educate Yourself:* Learn about adolescent development and the specific challenges today's teenagers face. Understanding their world builds empathy and improves your ability to respond appropriately.

- *Model Healthy Behavior:* Teens learn as much from how adults act as from what they say. Demonstrate respect, patience, and healthy conflict resolution in your interactions.

- *Maintain Confidentiality:* Respect privacy, but also know when to involve others if a teenager's safety is at risk. Transparency about these limits is important.

- *Encourage Strengths:* Highlight the teenager's gifts and achievements, no matter how small. Positive reinforcement brings a growth mindset and self-esteem.

The Ripple Effect of Safe Adults

The impact of safe adults stretches far beyond the individual teenager. When a young person experiences safety and support, they are more likely to thrive academically, socially, and emotionally. They become better equipped to resist negative peer influences and pursue their dreams.

Moreover, safe adults help break cycles of hurt and dysfunction. Many teenagers come from difficult backgrounds, and by providing a healthy, affirming relationship, teachers and mentors can introduce a different way of living and relating to others. These young people often grow up to become safe adults themselves, perpetuating a legacy of care and positive influence.

Challenges to Becoming a Safe Adult

While the role is deeply rewarding, becoming a safe adult is not without challenges. Teachers and mentors may struggle with heavy workloads, personal boundaries, or the fear of saying the wrong thing. There is also the risk of emotional burnout if the adult becomes too invested without adequate self-care.

It's important for safe adults to seek support and maintain their own well-being. Regular reflection, peer support, and professional development can strengthen their ability to sustain this role. Remember, being a safe adult doesn't mean having all the answers; it means being present, compassionate, and committed.

11.3 Practical Classroom Tools

Teachers and mentors play a vital role in shaping the lives of teenagers. Beyond imparting knowledge, they guide young people in navigating the complexities of adolescence, building character, responsibility, and encouraging personal growth. However, good intentions alone are not enough. To truly connect with and influence teenagers, educators must be equipped with practical tools that create a positive and engaging learning environment. This section explores some of the most effective classroom tools and techniques that teachers and mentors can use to reach teenagers in today's fast-paced and often challenging world.

Understanding the Teenage Mindset

Before studying specific tools, it is essential to understand the mindset of teenagers. Adolescence is a time of emotional, social, and cognitive changes. Teens crave independence but still need guidance; they desire respect but often struggle with self-confidence; they want to be heard but may have difficulty expressing themselves clearly. Recognizing this complex dynamic helps teachers tailor their approach and choose tools that resonate.

1. Building Relationships Through Active Listening

One of the simplest yet most powerful tools teachers have is **active listening**. When a teacher truly listens to a teenager without interrupting, judging, or immediately offering advice, it communicates respect and value.

Active listening involves:

- Giving full attention to the speaker

- Maintaining eye contact

- Nodding or using encouraging phrases

- Reflecting on what the student said for clarity.

This practice creates trust and openness, making students feel safe to share their thoughts and challenges. A mentor who listens well can often identify issues before they escalate and provide timely support.

2. Using Clear and Positive Communication

Teenagers respond better to clear, respectful, and positive communication rather than harsh criticism or vague commands. Teachers should aim to:

- Use *"I" statements* to express feelings without blaming (e.g., "I feel concerned when...")

- Give *specific feedback* rather than general comments (e.g., "You did a great job organizing your ideas in this essay.")

- Reinforce effort as much as achievement (e.g., "I noticed how hard you worked on this project.")

Clear communication helps prevent misunderstandings and builds confidence. It also models how teens can communicate effectively with peers and adults.

3. Incorporating Interactive Learning Tools

Teenagers today are digital natives, accustomed to interactive and multimedia experiences. Incorporating technology and hands-on activities can make learning more engaging:

- *Educational apps and online quizzes:* These provide instant feedback and gamify learning, which can motivate students.

- *Group projects and peer collaboration:* Working with others builds social skills and accountability.

- *Visual aids like charts, videos, and infographics:* These help explain complex concepts in an accessible way.

Balancing traditional teaching with interactive tools addresses different learning styles and keeps students interested.

4. Setting Clear Expectations and Consistent Boundaries

Teenagers flourish in environments where expectations and boundaries are clear and consistently enforced. Teachers and mentors can use practical tools such as:

- *Classroom rules displayed prominently:* Having clear rules visible reminds students of acceptable behavior.

- *Behavior charts or points systems:* These can encourage positive behavior and provide immediate consequences for missteps.

- *Routine and structure:* Predictable schedules help teens feel secure and manage time better.

Consistency in applying these tools helps students understand limits and develop self-discipline.

5. Encouraging Goal Setting and Self-Reflection

Helping teenagers set realistic goals and reflect on their progress empowers them to take ownership of their learning and personal development. Practical tools include:

- *Goal sheets or journals:* Teens write down academic or personal goals and track milestones.

- *Reflection prompts*: Questions like "What did I do well today?" or "What can I improve on?" encourage thoughtful self-assessment.

- *One-on-one mentoring sessions:* Provide space to discuss goals, challenges, and growth plans.

Goal setting builds motivation and teaches important life skills such as planning, perseverance, and self-evaluation.

6. Utilizing Positive Reinforcement

Positive reinforcement is a powerful tool to encourage desired behavior. Teachers can use:

- *Verbal praise:* Recognizing effort and achievement boosts self-esteem.

- *Reward systems:* Stickers, points, or small privileges can motivate students.

- *Public recognition:* Celebrating accomplishments during class or assemblies promotes a positive atmosphere.

Consistent positive reinforcement helps teenagers internalize good habits and strengthens their commitment to learning.

7. Incorporating Emotional Regulation Strategies

Since teenagers often experience heightened emotions, teachers and mentors can equip them with tools to manage feelings productively. Practical methods include:

- *Journaling or art projects:* Creative outlets for expressing emotions safely.

- *Conflict resolution training:* Role-playing scenarios to practice empathy and problem-solving.

When students learn to regulate their emotions, they are better able to focus and engage in class.

Practical classroom tools are essential for teachers and mentors to effectively guide teenagers through this transformative phase of life. By listening actively, communicating clearly, incorporating interactive learning, setting boundaries, encouraging goal setting, reinforcing positive behavior, and supporting emotional regulation, educators create an environment where teens can thrive. These tools do more than improve academic success; they build the character, resilience, and self-awareness teenagers need to navigate today's complex world and prepare for the future.

Chapter 12

Financial Education for Teens

12.1 Teaching Money Skills Early

In today's fast-paced and ever-changing world, understanding money is more important than ever, especially for teenagers. Financial education is not just about knowing how to spend or save money; it's about building lifelong skills that shape attitudes, decisions, and habits. Teaching money skills early equips teens with the tools they need to handle financial challenges confidently and wisely as they grow into adults.

Why Start Early?

The teenage years are a crucial time for forming habits and attitudes toward money. Many adults struggle with debt, overspending, or financial stress because they never learned basic money management skills when they were young. Starting financial education early can prevent costly mistakes later on, helping teens develop responsibility and independence.

When teens learn about money in their formative years, they gain:

- Confidence in managing their own finances;

- Understanding of the value of money and work;

- Ability to set financial goals and work toward them;

- Skills to avoid common pitfalls like overspending or falling into debt;

By teaching money skills early, parents, teachers, and mentors help young people build a foundation for a stable and secure future.

Core Money Skills for Teens

Budgeting

One of the most fundamental skills teens can learn is how to create and stick to a budget.

A budget is a plan for how to spend and save money.

Teaching teens to budget helps them understand that money is limited and must be managed wisely.

For example, if a teen receives an allowance or earns money from part-time work, they can divide their income into categories such as giving, saving, and spending. Encouraging them to track their expenses, even simple ones like snacks or subscriptions, builds awareness of where their money goes.

Tithing: Honouring God with What You Have

One important biblical principle that teenagers should begin to understand early in life is tithing. Tithing simply means giving one-tenth of your income or increase to God. This practice dates back to the time of Abraham (Genesis 14:20) and was reaffirmed in the law of Moses (Malachi 3:10). Though many teenagers don't have full-time jobs yet, they still receive pocket money, gifts, allowances, or even small earnings from part-time work, and these are opportunities to learn how to honor God with their resources.

Tithing teaches young people *responsibility, faith, and gratitude.* It helps them understand that all they have comes from God and that giving back to Him is an act of worship. When teenagers give their tithe, they learn to trust God as their Provider. It also builds a habit of generosity that carries into adulthood. God promises to bless those who tithe faithfully, not just financially, but in wisdom, protection, and provision (Malachi 3:10-12). Learning this principle early can help teens avoid greed and develop a giving heart, even in a world that encourages selfishness and materialism.

Saving

Saving is more than just putting money aside; it's about planning for future needs and emergencies. Teens should understand the importance of saving a portion of their income regularly, even if it's a small amount. This habit will serve them well when they want to buy something expensive or face unexpected costs.

Introduce concepts like setting short-term savings goals (e.g., saving for a new phone or a trip) and long-term goals (e.g., college or a car). Using tools like a piggy bank, savings account, or apps designed for young savers can make the process tangible and rewarding.

Spending Wisely

Teaching teens to spend wisely means helping them differentiate between wants and needs. It's easy to get caught up in advertising or peer pressure to buy the latest gadgets or fashion trends. Encouraging teens to pause and think critically before spending helps prevent impulsive purchases.

A simple rule to teach is the *"24-hour rule"*: wait 24 hours before making a non-essential purchase. This gives time to evaluate if the item is really needed or just an impulse.

Understanding Credit and Debt

While many teens might not yet use credit cards or loans, understanding how credit works and the dangers of debt is crucial. Teach them that borrowing money comes with responsibilities, such as paying back on time with interest.

Explain the risks of debt accumulation and how it can affect their finances, including credit scores, which can impact their ability to get loans or even rent an apartment.

Earning Money

Financial education also includes learning the value of earning money through work. Encouraging teens to take on part-time jobs, internships, or entrepreneurial activities teaches them discipline, responsibility, and the connection between work and income.

This experience also develops a strong work ethic and helps teens appreciate the money they have, making them less likely to spend carelessly.

How to Teach Money Skills Early

Lead by Example

Parents and adults are the first and most important teachers. Teens learn by watching how adults handle money. Open conversations about family budgeting, saving goals, and spending choices provide real-life lessons. Share stories of successes and mistakes to make the learning authentic and relatable.

Use Real Money Situations

Involve teens in practical money decisions. For example, take them grocery shopping and give them a budget to buy certain items. Let them plan for special occasions like birthdays or holidays. These hands-on experiences reinforce concepts better than abstract lessons.

Incorporate Technology

Many apps and online tools are designed to teach young people about money management. These tools can help teens track their income and expenses, set savings goals, and even invest in virtual stock markets. Using technology that teens already enjoy makes learning money skills engaging and fun.

Make It Part of the School Curriculum

Financial education should not be left to chance. Schools can play a vital role by including basic money management in their curriculum. Workshops, seminars, and projects focused on financial literacy prepare teens for real-world challenges and empower them with knowledge.

Encourage Open Dialogue

Create a safe space for teens to ask questions and discuss money openly without fear of judgment. Many teens feel uncertain about money topics. Encouraging openness builds confidence and removes taboos around finances.

The Long-Term Benefits

Teaching money skills early helps teenagers become responsible adults who can:

- Make informed financial decisions.

- Avoid debt traps and build good credit.

- Plan for big life goals like higher education, buying a home, or starting a family.

- Give generously and manage resources to bless others.

- Develop a mindset of abundance and stewardship rather than scarcity and fear.

Financial education is not just about money; it's about shaping character. It teaches patience, discipline, accountability, and planning qualities that benefit all areas of life.

12.2 Entrepreneurship and Budgeting

In today's fast-paced and ever-changing world, financial education has become essential for teenagers. Two of the most important aspects that teens can learn early on are entrepreneurship and budgeting. These skills not only help young people understand the value of money but also equip them with the mindset and tools to succeed independently in the future.

Understanding Entrepreneurship for Teens

Entrepreneurship is the ability to create, develop, and manage a business venture with the goal of making a profit. For teenagers, entrepreneurship is more than just starting a company; it is about developing problem-solving skills, creativity, responsibility, and resilience. The world is full of opportunities for young entrepreneurs, and many teenagers have already started small businesses ranging from lawn care, tutoring, and crafts to digital services such as social media management or content creation.

Why is entrepreneurship important for teens? First, it teaches valuable life lessons about work ethic and perseverance. Running a business, even a small one, requires planning, dedication, and learning from mistakes. Teens who engage in entrepreneurship also learn how to communicate effectively, manage time, and make decisions under pressure; all skills that are useful in any career.

Moreover, entrepreneurship fosters a growth mindset. Teens learn that challenges are opportunities to innovate and improve rather than obstacles. This mindset helps them develop confidence and independence, as they realize that they can create solutions and generate income on their own terms.

Parents, schools, and communities can support teenage entrepreneurship by encouraging creative ideas and providing resources such as mentorship, training programs, or access to microloans. The earlier teens get involved in entrepreneurship, the better prepared they will be for the financial realities of adult life.

The Basics of Budgeting for Teens

Budgeting is the process of planning how to allocate money for various expenses, savings, and sometimes investments. For teenagers, understanding budgeting is crucial because it helps them develop discipline and awareness about their spending habits. When teens learn to budget, they become more mindful about distinguishing needs from wants and managing limited resources wisely.

A simple way to start budgeting is by teaching teens to track their income and expenses. Income could come from allowances, part-time jobs, gifts, or business ventures. Expenses include everything from buying snacks and clothes to paying for transportation or entertainment. By keeping a record, teens can see where their money goes and identify areas where they can cut back or save more.

An effective budget divides money into categories such as:

- *Savings:* Setting aside a portion of income for future goals or emergencies.

- *Essentials:* Money spent on necessary items or services.

- *Wants:* Spending on non-essential items, which should be controlled.

- *Giving:* Some teens also choose to allocate a part of their income to charity or gifts, teaching generosity.

Learning to budget also helps teens avoid debt by encouraging them to live within their means. It builds financial responsibility and prepares them for managing bigger expenses like college fees, rent, or even buying a car in the future.

Combining Entrepreneurship and Budgeting

When teens combine entrepreneurship with budgeting, the benefits multiply. Running a small business gives teens hands-on experience with income and expenses, making budgeting more meaningful. For example, a teen who starts a lemonade stand or a social media consulting service must manage costs for supplies, advertising, and possibly taxes, while also keeping track of profits.

Entrepreneurial teens learn to budget for business needs and personal expenses, balancing between reinvesting in their venture and saving for personal goals. This experience builds financial literacy, teaching them to forecast income, set pricing strategies, and understand profit margins.

By managing a business budget, teens gain insight into real-world finance that goes far beyond classroom theory. They become more accountable and strategic with money. Many successful adult entrepreneurs credit their early teenage experiences with business and budgeting as critical to their later success.

Practical Tips for Teens Starting Out

- *Start Small and Simple:* Begin with a business idea that matches your skills and interests, like baking, crafts, tutoring, or digital services. Avoid complex ventures at first.

- *Create a Basic Budget:* Use a notebook or smartphone app to track your income and expenses regularly. Plan how much money you want to save versus spend.

- *Set Clear Goals:* Define what you want to achieve; whether it is saving for a gadget, funding college, or expanding your business. Goals provide motivation and direction.

- *Seek Guidance:* Talk to parents, teachers, or mentors who can offer advice on business and financial matters.

- *Keep it Legal and Ethical:* Ensure your business complies with local rules and treat customers with honesty and respect.

The Role of Schools and Communities

Schools and community organizations play a vital role in promoting financial education. Incorporating entrepreneurship and budgeting into the curriculum equips all teens with essential skills, regardless of their background. Workshops, clubs, competitions, and internships can provide practical experiences that make financial concepts tangible.

Involving parents in this education is also important. Open conversations about money at home can reinforce lessons learned elsewhere. Parents who model good financial habits encourage their teens to do the same.

Entrepreneurship and budgeting are two pillars of financial education that empower teenagers to take control of their financial futures. By learning how to create and manage a business alongside developing disciplined money management habits, teens build confidence, responsibility, and independence. These skills will serve them not only as individuals but also as contributors to their communities and economies.

Financial education is not just about numbers; it is about shaping a mindset that values hard work, smart decisions, and resilience. Investing time and effort into teaching teens about entrepreneurship and budgeting today will help create a generation of financially savvy adults who can thrive in an unpredictable world.

12.3 Saving, Investing, and Giving

Financial education is one of the most important life skills that teenagers can develop early on. Understanding how to manage money wisely sets a foundation for future independence, financial security, and even generosity. In this section, we will explore three crucial concepts: saving, investing, and giving. Each of these plays a vital role in shaping a balanced and responsible approach to money.

Saving: Building Your Financial Safety Net

Saving money is often the first step teenagers learn in financial education. Saving means setting aside a portion of your income or allowance instead of spending it immediately. It may sound simple, but the habit of saving is powerful.

Why should teens save money?

First, savings provide a safety net. Life is unpredictable; unexpected expenses like a broken phone, emergency travel, or a school trip can come up. Having money saved up helps you avoid stress and financial trouble in these moments.

Second, saving allows you to plan and achieve bigger goals. Whether you want to buy a bike, a laptop, or pay for a course or hobby, saving little by little over time makes these goals attainable. The earlier you start, the more time your money has to grow, thanks to a concept called compound interest (which we'll touch on shortly).

Practical tips for saving as a teen

- *Set a goal:* Know what you're saving for. This makes saving more meaningful and keeps you motivated.

- *Create a budget:* Track what you earn and spend each month. This helps you find money to save.

- *Pay yourself:* When you get money, immediately set aside a portion for savings before spending on anything else. Even 10% is a great start.

Use a separate account or a physical jar: Keeping your savings separate makes it less tempting to spend.

Saving isn't just about putting money away; it's about learning patience, self-control, and planning for the future.

Investing: Making Your Money Work for You

Once you have some savings, you can start thinking about investing. Investing means using your money to buy something that has the potential to grow in value or earn income over time. Unlike saving, where money usually sits in a bank account, investing puts your money to work.

For teenagers, investing might seem complicated or risky, but understanding the basics early on can lead to huge advantages later in life. The biggest benefit of investing is that your money can grow faster than if it's just saved in a low-interest account.

Common investment options

- *Stocks:* Buying shares of companies means you own a small part of that company. If the company does well, the value of your shares may increase.

- *Bonds:* Loans to companies or governments that pay you interest over time. They tend to be safer but offer lower returns.

- *Mutual funds/ETFs:* These are collections of many stocks and bonds, managed by professionals, which help spread out risk.

- *Savings accounts with interest:* While not technically an investment, some high-yield accounts pay better interest than standard ones.

A simple example of investing is buying stocks in a company you believe in. Over the years, the stock's value can increase, growing your initial investment. But remember, investments can also go down, so it's important to learn, be patient, and avoid risky "get-rich-quick" schemes.

Key investing principles for teens

- *Start early:* Thanks to compound interest, the earlier you start investing, the more time your money has to grow. Even small amounts add up over decades.

- *Learn and research:* Don't invest in something you don't understand. Take time to read and ask questions.

- *Diversify:* Don't put all your money in one place. Spreading investments reduces risk.

- *Be patient*: Investing is a long-term game. Avoid panic selling when markets fluctuate.

Consider starting with small amounts or simulated stock market games to practice investing skills.

Giving: The Joy and Power of Generosity

Financial education is not just about accumulating wealth; it's also about learning to give. Giving means using part of your money or resources to help others, support causes you care about, or invest in your community.

For many teens, the idea of giving away money they've worked hard for may feel strange; why give away money you've earned? But generosity is a powerful and fulfilling part of managing money well. It builds empathy, gratitude, and a sense of purpose beyond yourself.

Giving can take many forms:

- Donating money to charities or causes.

- Buying gifts for family or friends.

- Volunteering your time or skills.

- Supporting community projects or church activities.

Studies show that people who give regularly tend to be happier and more satisfied with life. Giving also teaches responsibility and breaks the cycle of selfishness that can come from focusing only on material things.

How to practice giving as a teen:

Set aside a fixed percentage of your income or allowance for giving: 10% is a common and meaningful amount.

Remember, giving is not just about money. Your time, talents, and encouragement are valuable gifts too.

By including giving in your financial education, you balance your own needs with the needs of others, becoming a thoughtful and generous adult.

Bringing It All Together: The Balanced Money Mindset

Saving, investing, and giving are not isolated activities; they form a balanced approach to money management. Here's how to think about them together:

- *Save* for short-term needs and emergencies so you can avoid debt and be prepared.

- *Invest* for long-term growth and building wealth over time.

- *Give* to make a positive impact and live a meaningful life beyond personal gain.

This balance helps teens develop financial wisdom that goes beyond just making or spending money. It builds character, self-discipline, and a mindset that values security, growth, and generosity.

Final Thoughts for Teens

Money is a tool. By learning to save, invest, and give wisely, you take control of your financial future and build habits that will benefit you for life.

Start small, be consistent, and remember that financial education is a journey, not a destination. With knowledge, patience, and a generous heart, you can create a future where money serves you, your family, and your community well.

Chapter 13

Supporting Their Mental and Emotional Health

The teenage years are a crucial time of growth and change, filled with both exciting possibilities and significant challenges. Adolescents navigate physical changes, identity development, social pressures, academic demands, and emerging independence. These factors can profoundly impact their mental and emotional well-being. Supporting teenagers' mental health is therefore essential; not only to help them cope with difficulties but also to empower them to thrive.

Mental health is more than the absence of illness; it includes emotional resilience, a positive sense of self, and the ability to manage stress and relationships effectively. Many teenagers today face increased risks to their mental well-being, including anxiety, depression, loneliness, and low self-esteem. These issues can arise from bullying, family conflicts, social media pressures, academic stress, and uncertain futures.

In response, parents, educators, community leaders, and churches need to proactively support teenagers' mental and emotional health. Among the most effective ways to do this is by creating *safe spaces*, environments where teenagers feel accepted, understood, and free from judgment. Safe spaces allow young people to express themselves authentically, explore their feelings, and find encouragement and guidance.

13.1 Creating Safe Spaces

Creating safe spaces is about more than providing a physical location. It is about cultivating an atmosphere of trust, respect, and acceptance that supports the whole teenager, mind, body, soul, and spirit. When young people sense that they are truly safe, they are more likely to open up, share their struggles, and seek help before problems escalate.

Here are key elements to consider when establishing safe spaces for teenagers:

1. **Non-Judgmental Acceptance**

   Teenagers often fear being judged or misunderstood. They may hesitate to share their true feelings or experiences if they worry about criticism or rejection. Safe spaces must be free from judgment, where young people know they can be vulnerable without fear.

   This means listening actively and empathetically, affirming their feelings even when you don't fully agree, and respecting their perspectives. Adults should avoid dismissive comments or quick solutions. Instead, they should encourage honest conversations, showing that every emotion is valid and worth exploring.

2. **Confidentiality and Trust**

   Trust is the foundation of any safe space. Teenagers must feel confident that what they share will be kept confidential, unless there is a risk of harm to themselves or others. Clear guidelines about confidentiality help build this trust.

Adults can reinforce trust by being reliable and consistent, following through on promises, and respecting boundaries. When trust is established, teenagers are more likely to seek support, knowing they won't be exposed or betrayed.

3. **Inclusivity and Respect for Diversity**

Teenagers come from diverse backgrounds and experiences. A safe space embraces this diversity, whether related to race, religion, socio-economic status, or abilities.

An inclusive environment *celebrates* differences rather than merely *tolerating* them. It challenges stereotypes and combats discrimination. For many teenagers, especially those who feel marginalized, safe spaces are a rare refuge where they can be their authentic selves.

4. **Physical and Emotional Safety**

A safe space must be physically secure, free from threats of violence or harm. It should also support emotional safety, where teenagers feel comfortable expressing difficult feelings without ridicule or punishment.

This includes creating clear rules for respectful behavior and addressing bullying or exclusion immediately. Emotional safety means providing a calm, supportive environment that encourages healing and growth.

5. **Access to Support and Resources**

Safe spaces should connect teenagers to appropriate support, whether that's peer support, counseling, mentorship, or educational resources. It's important that young people know help is available and accessible.

Providing information about mental health, coping strategies, and how to seek help empowers teenagers to take charge of their well-being. Safe spaces can also offer practical activities that promote mental health, such as mindfulness exercises, creative expression, and group discussions.

Practical Ways to Create Safe Spaces for Teenagers

Whether in schools, churches, youth clubs, or homes, there are many practical steps adults can take to create safe spaces:

- *Listen Without Interrupting:* Give teenagers your full attention, show genuine interest, and avoid jumping to conclusions or giving unsolicited advice.

- *Use Affirming Language:* Encourage teenagers by acknowledging their strengths and efforts, not just their challenges.

- *Establish Clear Guidelines:* Co-create rules with teenagers about respectful communication and confidentiality to build mutual respect.

- *Encourage Peer Support:* Facilitate group activities where teens can share experiences and support one another in a structured and positive way.

- *Train Adults:* Ensure teachers, youth leaders, and parents receive training on adolescent mental health, active listening, and trauma-informed care.

- *Provide Creative Outlets:* Offer art, music, drama, or writing opportunities that allow emotional expression in nonverbal ways.

- *Create Comfortable Physical Spaces:* Arrange seating in circles, use calming colors and lighting, and provide cozy areas for small group chats or private conversations.

- *Be Present and Available:* Consistently make yourself available and approachable to teenagers, so they know they have someone to turn to.

The Role of the Church in Safe Spaces

The Church has a unique opportunity to create safe spaces rooted in unconditional love and acceptance. Many teenagers struggle with questions of identity, purpose, and belonging, areas where faith can offer grounding and hope.

Church youth groups and ministries can model safe spaces by demonstrating grace and compassion, teaching about God's love, and offering pastoral care. When young people feel spiritually safe, they grow in confidence and resilience. They learn to integrate their faith with mental health practices, finding peace amid life's challenges.

Supporting teenagers' mental and emotional health is a vital task that requires intentional effort and sensitivity. Creating safe spaces is a foundational step in this process where young people feel valued, heard, and empowered. These environments nurture emotional resilience, build trust, and bring healthy relationships.

When we provide safe spaces for teenagers, we not only help them overcome present difficulties but also equip them with the skills and confidence to navigate the complexities of adulthood. In a world that often feels chaotic and overwhelming, safe spaces are a beacon of hope, healing, and growth.

13.2 Knowing When to Get Professional Help

Teenagers today face a unique set of challenges that can deeply affect their mental and emotional health. As parents, teachers, mentors, or caregivers, supporting them effectively means not only offering love and guidance but also recognizing when their struggles go beyond what we can handle on our own. One of the most critical skills in supporting teens is knowing when it's time to seek professional help.

Mental health professionals, such as counselors, psychologists, psychiatrists, and social workers, are trained to understand and treat the complex emotions and behaviors teens experience. While many problems can be managed through family support, good communication, and healthy lifestyle habits, there are moments when professional intervention is necessary to help teens navigate their difficulties safely and effectively.

Signs That Indicate Professional Help May Be Needed

Recognizing when a teenager needs professional help can be challenging because many teens naturally experience mood swings, stress, and anxiety. However, certain signs suggest that their struggles may be more serious than typical adolescent challenges:

- *Persistent sadness or irritability:* If a teen feels overwhelmingly sad or irritable for weeks or months without improvement, it may be a sign of depression.

- *Withdrawal from family and friends:* When a teenager isolates themselves socially and loses interest in activities they once enjoyed, it signals emotional distress.

- *Decline in academic performance:* A sudden drop in grades, difficulty concentrating, or lack of motivation may reflect deeper mental health issues.

- *Changes in sleeping or eating habits:* Insomnia, excessive sleeping, drastic weight loss or gain can be physical indicators of emotional problems.

- *Talk of self-harm:* Any mention of self-injury or hopelessness should be taken very seriously and addressed immediately.

- *Unexplained physical complaints:* Frequent headaches, stomach-aches, or other pains without a medical cause may be linked to emotional distress.

- *Risky or destructive behavior:* Substance abuse, reckless driving, or dangerous acts can be cries for help that require urgent attention.

When these signs are present, it is crucial not to dismiss them or assume they will simply "pass with time." Timely professional help can make a significant difference in a teenager's recovery and long-term well-being.

Barriers to Seeking Professional Help

Despite the importance of professional support, many teens and families hesitate to reach out. Understanding the barriers that prevent getting help can improve how we approach the situation:

- *Stigma:* There is still a social stigma surrounding mental health issues that can make teens feel embarrassed or fearful about being judged.

- *Lack of awareness:* Some parents or teens may not fully recognize the severity of the problem or know where to find help.

- *Fear of loss of control:* Teens may worry that seeing a counselor means losing privacy or being forced to talk about things they aren't ready to share.

- *Cost and access:* Professional mental health care can be expensive or hard to access in some areas.

- *Cultural beliefs:* Certain cultures may discourage talking openly about emotional struggles or seeking external help.

As caregivers, it is essential to address these barriers with empathy and patience. Encouraging open conversations about mental health, normalizing seeking help, and providing information about accessible resources can break down these walls.

How to Approach the Conversation

Starting a conversation about professional help can be difficult. Teenagers may feel defensive or reluctant to open up. Here are some practical tips for approaching this sensitive topic:

- Choose a calm, private time to talk where you won't be interrupted.

- Express your concern with kindness and without blame: "I've noticed you seem not so happy lately, and I want to help."

- Listen actively and validate their feelings: "It's okay to feel this way; you don't have to go through it alone, let us find a solution together."

- Reassure them that seeking help is a sign of strength, not weakness.

- Offer to support them in finding a professional and even accompany them to the first appointment.

- Respect their pace and willingness, but emphasize the importance of taking steps toward help.

What to Expect from Professional Help

Understanding what happens in professional care can ease fear and resistance. Depending on the situation, a professional may:

- Conduct an initial assessment to understand the teen's emotional state.

- Offer counseling sessions to teach coping skills, improve communication, and work through difficult emotions.

- In some cases, recommend medication to help manage symptoms of depression, anxiety, or other disorders.

- Provide family therapy to improve home support and relationships.

- Develop a safety plan if the teen has evil thoughts or behaviors.

Remember, the goal of professional help is to empower the teen to heal and grow, equipping them with tools to face life's challenges more confidently.

The Role of Ongoing Support

Professional help is often a key step, but it works best alongside ongoing support from family, friends, and community. Encouraging healthy routines, maintaining open communication, and modeling emotional resilience create a safe environment where teens feel valued and understood.

Helping teens build strong mental and emotional health is a team effort. Recognizing when professional help is needed and acting with compassion can save lives and change futures.

13.3 Building Confidence and Self-Love

Many teenagers struggle with feelings of insecurity, self-doubt, and low self-esteem. Building confidence and self-love is not just a nice-to-have; it is essential for their mental and emotional health. When young people learn to appreciate their own worth and believe in their abilities, they become better equipped to face life's obstacles, make healthy decisions, and develop positive relationships.

Understanding Confidence and Self-Love

Confidence is the belief in one's abilities and qualities. It allows teenagers to take on new challenges, speak up for themselves, and pursue their goals without fear of failure. Self-love, on the other hand, is a deeper and more foundational concept. It involves accepting oneself fully: flaws, mistakes, and all; and treating oneself with kindness and respect. Self-love creates the inner security that shields teenagers from harmful criticism and comparison.

Yet, many teens today face pressure from social media, academic expectations, peer groups, and even family dynamics that can erode their self-confidence. They see curated images of "perfect" lives, "ideal" bodies, and flawless achievements that are often unrealistic. Without guidance and support, teens may begin to believe they are not good enough or worthy of love.

Why Building Confidence Matters

- Confidence affects every part of a teenager's life. When they feel confident:

- They try new things without fear of judgment. This helps them discover their talents and interests.

- They speak up for their needs, boundaries, and beliefs, making healthier relationships.

- They cope better with criticism, seeing it as an opportunity to learn rather than evidence of inadequacy.

- They experience less anxiety and stress because they trust in their ability to handle challenges.

- On the contrary, a lack of confidence can lead to withdrawal, depression, and even risky behaviors as teens attempt to mask their insecurities.

Practical Ways to Build Confidence

Building confidence is a process that takes time, encouragement, and practice. Here are some ways parents, teachers, mentors, and the teens themselves can build confidence:

- **Celebrate Effort, Not Just Results**
  Encourage teens to focus on the process rather than the outcome. Praise their hard work, persistence and willingness to try. This mindset helps them understand that mistakes are part of learning and growth.

- **Set Achievable Goals**
  Help teens set realistic and attainable goals. When they accomplish these, no matter how small, it boosts their sense of capability and motivation to pursue bigger goals.

- **Encourage Positive Self-Talk**
  Teens often have a critical inner voice that sometimes repeats negative messages. Teach them to recognize and challenge these thoughts by replacing them with positive affirmations. For example, instead of "I'm not good enough," they can say, "I am learning and growing every day."

- **Promote Strengths and Talents**
  Every teenager has unique gifts and skills. Encourage them to explore their interests and hobbies, whether it's art, sports, music, or academics. Success and enjoyment in these areas build a strong foundation of self-worth.

- **Model Confidence and Self-Love**
  Adults play a crucial role by demonstrating self-respect and confidence in their own lives. When teens see healthy behaviors in the people they trust, they are more likely to adopt them.

- **Provide Supportive Feedback**
  Offer constructive and kind feedback that focuses on improvement rather than criticism. Let teens know that you believe in their potential and that mistakes do not define their value.

Cultivating Self-Love in Teenagers

Self-love goes beyond confidence; it means nurturing a positive relationship with oneself. Here are some ways to encourage self-love:

- **Teach Compassion**
  Help teens treat themselves with the same kindness they would offer a friend. When they feel down or make mistakes, encourage them to respond with understanding rather than harsh judgment.

- **Encourage Healthy Boundaries**
  Self-love means recognizing and protecting one's emotional and physical limits. Teach teens to say no when necessary and to prioritize their well-being.

- **Promote Mindfulness and Gratitude**
  Practices such as journaling about things they are grateful for or spending a few moments each day in quiet reflection help teens connect with their inner selves and appreciate life beyond external validation.

- **Help Them Develop a Personal Identity**
  Support teens in exploring their values, beliefs, and passions. When they understand who they are and what matters most to them, they build a stronger sense of self.

Help teens navigate social media and peer influence wisely

While social media can offer connection and inspiration, it can also undermine confidence and self-love. Teens often compare themselves to idealized images and may feel pressured to conform to unrealistic standards. Helping teens navigate social media wisely is essential:

- Encourage *critical thinking* about what they see online.

- Promote *digital detoxes* to reduce exposure to negative content.

- Support *real-life friendships* that provide genuine acceptance and encouragement.

Peers also influence self-esteem greatly during adolescence. Encourage teens to build friendships that uplift and support their confidence, and help them recognize when relationships are harmful or draining.

Building confidence and self-love in teenagers is an ongoing journey that requires patience, encouragement, and intentional support. When young people develop these qualities, they gain a powerful foundation for mental and emotional health. They learn to face life's challenges with courage and resilience, embrace their unique identity, and grow into healthy, fulfilled adults. As parents, mentors, and Church members, we have the responsibility and privilege to guide them on this vital path.

Chapter 14

The Power of Community and Positive Peer Influence

14.1 Youth Groups, Safe Hangouts, and Clubs

When teenagers belong to a supportive community, it can significantly shape their self-esteem, choices, and overall well-being. This chapter explores how youth groups, safe hangouts, and youth organizations provide a positive environment where teenagers can flourish and experience the power of positive peer influence.

The Need for Community Among Teenagers

Adolescence is a critical period when young people are learning who they are and where they fit in the world. One of the deepest human needs during this phase is belonging. Teenagers naturally seek connection with others their age to share experiences, express themselves, and find acceptance. When this need is met within a positive community, it provides a protective buffer against many of the risks associated with adolescence, such as peer pressure to engage in harmful behaviors, feelings of isolation, or emotional distress.

The power of community lies not just in having others around but in belonging to a group that encourages growth, supports healthy choices, and provides mentors and role models. Teenagers in such environments often develop better social skills, experience higher self-confidence, and show improved academic and emotional outcomes.

Youth Groups: More Than Just Meetings

Youth groups, whether organized through churches, schools, or community centers, offer teenagers a structured space to connect with peers who share similar values and interests. These groups often meet regularly for discussions, activities, service projects, and fun events that bring a sense of belonging and purpose.

Beyond socializing, youth groups create opportunities for teenagers to explore their faith, values, and goals in a safe and supportive setting. Leaders and adult mentors play a crucial role in guiding discussions, helping young people navigate difficult questions, and modeling positive behavior. In such groups, teenagers can openly talk about the challenges they face, pressure, mental health struggles, and family issues, without fear of judgment.

Moreover, youth groups often encourage service to others, helping teens develop empathy and a sense of responsibility. Participating in community service projects or outreach programs connects young people to the larger world and teaches them the value of giving back.

Safe Hangouts: Spaces to Belong and Be

Safe hangouts are informal, welcoming places where teenagers can gather to relax, have fun, and be themselves without fear of bullying or exclusion. These might be community centers, youth cafes, or after-school programs designed to offer positive alternatives to potentially harmful environments like unsupervised streets or internet spaces filled with negative influences.

Creating safe hangouts means providing a space that is physically safe and emotionally supportive. Staff or volunteers trained in youth development can help maintain a respectful atmosphere, resolve conflicts, and encourage positive interactions. These places often provide recreational activities, creative outlets such as art and music, spaces to sing worship songs together, or simply a welcoming environment to connect with friends.

For many teenagers, having a safe place to spend time after school or on weekends makes a tremendous difference. It reduces feelings of loneliness, discouragement, and boredom, which can sometimes lead to risky behaviors. Safe hangouts also encourage healthy socializing and help teens build friendships that reinforce positive identity and choices.

Youth Organizations and Extracurricular Activities: Developing Identity and Skills

Youth clubs and extracurricular activities, whether sports teams, drama clubs, debate groups, or hobby-based organizations, play a vital role in the healthy development of teenagers. These groups help teens discover and develop their talents, interests, and leadership skills.

Participation in youth clubs brings a sense of achievement and belonging. When teenagers work together toward a common goal, such as winning a tournament or producing a play, they learn teamwork, discipline, and perseverance. These experiences build confidence and self-worth.

Additionally, youth clubs often attract diverse groups of teenagers, encouraging inclusion and breaking down social barriers. This diversity allows young people to broaden their perspectives, build empathy, and develop communication skills with different types of people.

Being part of a team also often provides a built-in support system. The friendships and camaraderie formed here can serve as a strong positive influence, helping teenagers make healthy decisions and avoid negative peer pressure.

The Impact of Godly Friendships

One of the most powerful aspects of community and group involvement is positive peer influence. Teenagers are highly influenced by their friends and peers. When surrounded by peers who model kindness, respect, responsibility, and healthy habits, young people are more likely to adopt those good behaviors themselves.

Positive peer influence works both ways; it can help reduce risky behaviors like drug use, bullying, and truancy, while promoting positive habits such as studying, volunteering, and engaging in creative pursuits. Teenagers in supportive groups often feel motivated to reach their potential because they see their peers doing the same.

This effect extends beyond individual growth; positive peer groups can contribute to a culture of encouragement, accountability, and shared success. When teens support one another in setting and achieving goals, it creates a powerful environment where good choices become the norm.

Building Strong Communities for Today's Teenagers

The challenges teenagers face today can feel overwhelming, but the power of community offers hope and strength. Youth groups, safe hangouts, and youth clubs provide the foundation for healthy peer relationships and positive influences that help teens navigate adolescence successfully.

By investing in these communities, whether as parents, educators, mentors, or leaders, we create environments where young people can belong, grow, and thrive. This not only benefits individual teenagers but also builds stronger families, schools, and societies for the future.

14.2 Role Models and Mentorship Programs

Teenagers today are navigating a complex world filled with pressures and expectations that are often contradictory. They are exposed to countless voices, including social media influencers, celebrities, peers, and even algorithms. In this noisy environment, many young people are searching for someone to look up to; someone who embodies integrity, strength, resilience, and hope. That is why positive role models and structured mentorship programs are not just helpful; they are essential.

A role model is more than just someone who sets a good example. A role model is a living testimony of what is possible. When a teenager sees someone who has faced challenges, overcome adversity, and made wise choices, they begin to believe that they, too, can succeed. It's not about perfection; it's about authenticity.

Teenagers are not inspired by people who pretend to be flawless; they are drawn to those who are real, who have made mistakes and grown from them.

In communities where strong role models are present, whether that be a youth leader, a teacher, a coach, a parent, or a pastor, young people tend to flourish. These figures often become mirrors of what is possible, showing teens that a life of purpose, discipline, and faith is attainable. Role models provide a clear contrast to the destructive examples often celebrated in pop culture: some celebrities who promote self-centeredness, violence, and immorality.

The Church must rise to the occasion. We have a rich legacy of Godly men and women who can serve as mentors and examples. However, this requires intentionality. A teenager will not automatically follow a positive influence; they must be reached, engaged, and walked alongside. Mentorship programs are one way to do this effectively.

What Is Mentorship?

Mentorship is the act of guiding someone with less experience toward growth and maturity. It is a relationship, not a program.

While structured mentorship can involve scheduled meetings, goal-setting, and accountability, the heart of mentorship is love and investment. A mentor says, "I see value in you, and I am willing to give my time to help you become who God created you to be."

There are different types of mentorships:

- Some are formal, such as youth development programs organized by churches or schools.

- Others are informal and may grow naturally between a teen and a trusted adult. Both are valuable.

What matters most is consistency. Teenagers crave stability. A mentor who shows up regularly becomes a safe place, a sounding board, and a steady example.

Benefits of Mentorship Programs

- *Increased Confidence and Self-Worth*
  Many teens struggle with insecurity. A mentor can affirm their worth, speak life into their identity, and help them see themselves through God's Eyes. Knowing someone believes in them is often the turning point for a young person.

- *Improved Decision-Making*
  With a mentor's guidance, teens are less likely to make impulsive decisions or follow the wrong crowd. They learn to ask questions, weigh options, and seek wise counsel. Mentorship helps young people build the character needed for adult life.

- *Spiritual Growth*
  A Christian mentor leads by example in prayer, Bible reading, church participation, and Godly living. Through one-on-one discipleship, teens can deepen their relationship with God, gain a deeper understanding of Scripture, and learn to walk by faith.

- *Direction and Vision*
  Mentors help young people discover their gifts, passions, and purpose. Through encouragement and exposure to new ideas, teenagers begin to dream beyond their current situation. Mentors can connect them to opportunities and networks that lead to growth.

Characteristics of an Effective Role Model or Mentor

- *Integrity:* Teens are quick to detect hypocrisy. A mentor must live what they teach, even in private.

- *Empathy:* Understanding the struggles of adolescence is key. Judgment shuts doors; compassion opens them.

- *Faithfulness:* Consistent presence matters more than big words or flashy gestures. Being available builds trust.

- *Courage:* Sometimes mentors must challenge teens, speak hard truths, or confront bad behavior in love.

- *Prayerfulness:* A Godly mentor intercedes for their protégés, trusting God to do the deep work of transformation.

Creating a Culture of Mentorship in the Church

If we are to see our teenagers grow into strong, faith-filled adults, mentorship must become a culture, not a one-time project. Every Church can begin with a small group of willing adults committed to investing in the next generation. Training sessions, prayer meetings for youth, and intergenerational activities can help create connections.

Teens can also mentor each other. Peer-to-peer mentorship is powerful, especially when guided by adult oversight. Older teens can walk with younger ones, sharing their experiences and modeling how to live wisely. This also builds leadership skills and deepens their own faith.

Final Thoughts

The world is full of the wrong kind of influencers, and many teenagers are following those voices because they have not been given a better alternative. The Church, families, and community leaders must rise up and become visible, approachable, and faithful mentors. Every teenager needs someone who says, "I believe in you, and I will walk with you."

Let us pray and act. Let us build mentorship programs, invest in youth, and raise up a new generation of Godly role models who will influence the world, not be shaped by it. The power of community and positive peer influence is real, and with God's help, we can use it to turn hearts, transform lives, and equip teenagers to fulfill their destiny.

14.3 Encouraging Leadership and Service

Teenagers are not only the future; they are also the *now*. Within every young person lies the potential for greatness, but many times, that potential lies dormant because no one has called it out. One of the greatest gifts we can give teenagers is the opportunity to lead and serve. When teenagers are trusted with responsibility and invited into leadership and service roles, their confidence grows, their values are shaped, and their impact multiplies.

Discovering the Leader Within

Leadership is not about titles; it's about influence. Every teenager has influence in their circle, whether it's among friends, classmates, siblings, or even online. When teens recognize that their choices and words can affect others, they begin to see that they are already leading, whether they mean to or not. The key is to help them lead intentionally.

Many teenagers shy away from leadership because they equate it with perfection. They feel unqualified. But leadership is not about having all the answers; it is about taking initiative and caring enough to step forward. Encouraging teens to lead in small ways, like organizing a school project, initiating prayer at youth group, helping a new student, or leading a worship session, helps build leadership muscles over time.

We must train teenagers to see leadership as servanthood. Jesus said, "Whoever wants to become great among you must be your servant" (Matthew 20:26). This flips the world's view of leadership upside down. True leaders serve others, not for applause, but to uplift others and glorify God. When teens learn to lead by serving, they become change-makers in their schools, homes, and communities.

Opportunities for Service

Teens need platforms where they can put their energy, creativity, and passion to work. Yet, in many environments, teenagers are only expected to be passive participants. We must create spaces at church, in school, and in the community, where they can serve meaningfully.

Service opportunities help teenagers look beyond themselves. When a teen visits a home for the elderly, helps distribute food to the needy, joins a clean-up campaign, or volunteers at an after-school program, their worldview expands. They begin to see that their life has purpose.

Service grounds them. It gives them a sense of responsibility and fulfillment that partying, social media, or material things can never offer.

We should also remember that not all teens will serve in the same way. Some are naturally outgoing and will lead teams, preach, or organize events. Others may be more reserved but can serve quietly and effectively through art, writing, media, hospitality, or technical support. It is important to guide them to serve in line with their gifts and passions.

Leadership Starts with Discipleship

One of the most powerful models of encouraging leadership and service is seen in how The Lord Jesus trained His disciples. He didn't just lecture them; He lived with them, walked with them, gave them assignments, corrected them in love, and sent them out with authority. This is the kind of intentional mentorship teens need today.

Every teenager should be discipled, not just taught, but walked with. Youth leaders, pastors, parents, and mature believers must see themselves as mentors. Through intentional discipleship, teens can be taught integrity, spiritual maturity, and character development, which are all necessary ingredients for Godly leadership.

When we disciple young people, we also help them make better decisions about the voices they listen to. Peer pressure can push teenagers into destructive behaviors, but peer *influence* can also become a powerful force for good. A teenager who is discipled well can become a positive peer leader, drawing others away from compromise and toward purpose.

Building a Culture of Encouragement

To encourage leadership and service among teenagers, we must build a culture of encouragement. Teens will rise to expectations when they know they are believed in. A simple, sincere statement like "I see leadership in you," or "You handled that very well, keep going," can go a long way in helping a young person step into purpose.

Churches can set up youth councils, mentoring programs, or teen-led events. Schools can allow student-led initiatives, clubs, or service projects. Parents can give their children roles at home that carry responsibility, like helping younger siblings, managing certain household tasks, or organizing family devotions. These consistent opportunities help develop reliability and initiative.

We must also celebrate service, not just talent or popularity. When teens are praised only for beauty, grades, or sports performance, we may unintentionally promote a culture of performance over purpose. But when we celebrate acts of service, humility, faith, and consistency, we elevate the kind of leadership that truly transforms lives.

Raising Servant Leaders for the Kingdom

Encouraging teenagers to serve is not about making them busy; it's about preparing them for destiny. Many of the world's most influential Christians- pastors, authors, entrepreneurs, and missionaries started their journey as teenagers, doing small things with faithfulness. When teens serve with the right heart, they often receive divine direction about their life's purpose.

Let us not underestimate what God can do through a willing teenager. As Scripture says in 1 Timothy 4:12, *"Let no one despise your youth, but be an example to the believers in word, in conduct, in love, in spirit, in faith, in purity."* Teenagers can lead with excellence when we entrust them with real responsibility, walk with them patiently, and challenge them lovingly.

They are not too young to serve. They are not too inexperienced to lead. They simply need to be seen, supported, and stirred up. A teenager on fire for God, with a servant's heart and a leader's spirit, is a powerful tool for revival in this generation.

Chapter 15

Helping Teens Discover Purpose

15.1 Guiding them to their gifts and calling

Every teenager is born with God-given gifts, and these gifts are not random. They are clues to their calling. Romans 11:29 says, *"For the gifts and the calling of God are irrevocable."* This means that even if a teen is currently struggling, distracted, or feeling lost, their purpose is still intact. As mentors, teachers, parents, and spiritual leaders, our role is to help them discover and develop these gifts.

Start With Listening

Many teenagers don't even know they have gifts because no one has taken the time to observe or affirm what they do well. Begin by listening. What do they talk about passionately? What are they drawn to? What do others naturally ask them to help with? Sometimes the answer is hidden in what they do effortlessly: drawing, speaking, organizing, caring for others, solving problems, or defending those who are treated unfairly.

Use the Word of God

The Bible is filled with examples of young people who discovered their calling early. David was anointed king while still a teenager tending sheep (1 Samuel 16). Joseph received prophetic dreams in his youth (Genesis 37). Mary, the mother of Jesus, was a young woman who embraced her divine assignment. Share these stories with teens and show them that age is not a limitation to purpose.

Encourage them to pray and ask God to reveal their gifts. Lead them through scriptures like 1 Corinthians 12 and Romans 12, which outline spiritual gifts. Help them understand that their talents are not for fame or popularity, but to serve others and glorify God.

Create Opportunities for Service

A gift only grows when used. The Church and community can play a key role by providing safe spaces for teens to serve and explore. Let the musically inclined join the worship team, the tech-savvy teens help with media, and the bold ones lead prayers or youth Bible studies. Give them real responsibilities, not just entertainment.

You don't discover purpose in a classroom alone; you discover it by *doing*. When teens are involved in real ministry and service, their eyes begin to open to what they love, what they're good at, and where God is leading them.

Affirmation and Correction

Guidance involves both encouragement and redirection. When teens show signs of a gift, affirm it publicly and privately. When they misuse their gifts or act out of immaturity, correct them in love. Purpose discovery is a journey, and mistakes are part of the process. The goal is not perfection yet, but *progress*.

Encourage Vision Beyond Career

Many teens associate purpose only with a future career. While jobs and professions are part of life, purpose is bigger. A teenager may become a doctor, but their purpose might be to bring healing to the broken-hearted through kindness. A teen who loves fashion might be called to influence culture with modesty and creativity.

Help them see that their gifts are not just tools to make money but to fulfill destiny. When purpose is rooted in God's Kingdom, their identity becomes stronger, and their decisions become clearer.

Helping teenagers discover their purpose is one of the greatest gifts we can offer them. It protects them from comparison, confusion, and compromise. Purpose gives direction, identity, and fulfillment. Let us be a generation of parents, pastors, mentors, and teachers who not only tell teens what *not* to do, but who walk with them until they discover who God created them to be.

By guiding them to their gifts and calling, we prepare them not just for success, but for significance.

15.2 Helping Them Dream Big

Dreams are the language of destiny. When teenagers are encouraged to dream, they begin to imagine possibilities beyond their present circumstances. Yet, many teens have stopped dreaming. Life's challenges, broken homes, low self-esteem, or negative words from authority figures may have crushed their ability to see a brighter future. But one word of encouragement, one moment of inspiration, can rekindle the fire of hope and awaken a God-sized dream in a young heart.

Dreaming big doesn't mean chasing selfish ambition; it means aligning with the vision God has for their lives. Big dreams are born when teenagers understand that God can do "exceedingly abundantly above all that we ask or think" (Ephesians 3:20). They begin to believe that they can be used by God to bring change, lead others, write books, build businesses, preach the Gospel, or become Godly leaders in whatever field they choose.

1. Speak Life Over Their Future

Many teens are not dreaming big simply because no one told them they could. Speak prophetically into their lives. Tell them what you see in them. Call out their potential. Remind them that their background does not determine their destiny. Say things like:

- "God has great plans for your life."

- "You can do all things through Christ."

- "Don't settle. You were born to make a difference."

Words of life can break chains of limitations and spark a vision for the future.

2. Share Biblical Examples

Teenagers in the Bible dreamed big and changed history. Joseph had dreams of leadership even as a teenager. David was a young shepherd boy when he was anointed king. Esther was a young girl who saved a nation. Timothy was a young pastor mentored by Paul. These examples show teenagers that God uses young people to do big things.

Use these stories to help teens understand that their age is not a barrier to greatness. God doesn't wait until people are 30 or 40 to begin using them. He wants to start shaping their future now.

3. Create Environments for Dreaming

Help teens step away from constant entertainment and enter spaces where they can reflect, pray, write, plan, and dream. Organize youth retreats, quiet prayer moments, or even vision board activities. Encourage them to write down what they believe God is calling them to do. Ask questions like:

- What do you love doing?

- What problems do you want to solve?

- What kind of future would make you feel fulfilled?

- How can your gifts be used for God's glory?

When teens begin to visualize and articulate their dreams, those dreams begin to grow.

4. Expose Them to Bigger Possibilities

Sometimes teens can only dream as far as their environment allows. If no one around them has ever started a business, traveled, written a book, or gone to university, it's difficult for them to imagine doing those things themselves. But when you take them on mission trips, invite guest speakers, or connect them with mentors who have gone further, it expands their thinking.

Exposure breeds desire. If they can see it, they can start to believe it. Open their eyes to the vastness of God's world and the many ways they can serve Him.

5. Pray With Them and For Them

Dreams that are born in prayer are powerful and sustainable. Help teenagers develop a lifestyle of praying about their future. Teach them how to ask God for direction, how to listen for His voice, and how to surrender their will. Lay hands on them and declare God's Word over them.

When a dream is birthed in the presence of God, it becomes a divine assignment; not just a good idea. And God will provide the strength, resources, and open doors to fulfill what He has placed in their hearts.

Final Encouragement

Helping teenagers discover their purpose and dream big is one of the greatest investments we can make. When they begin to see themselves the way God sees them: chosen, loved, gifted, and powerful, they rise above insecurity, confusion, and fear. They stop wasting time and start preparing for impact.

Let's not underestimate what God can do through a teenager who is fully surrendered and passionately pursuing a big dream. One dream can ignite a generation. One vision can spark revival. One teenager can shift a nation.

Encourage them. Guide them. Believe in them. Help them dream big, because God has big plans for them.

15.3 Turning Pain into Power

Teenagers today face an overwhelming mix of pressures; academic expectations, family struggles, peer influence, and emotional wounds from rejection, abuse, or disappointment. Many young people walk around with invisible scars. Some have been abandoned by parents, bullied by classmates for simply being themselves. Others battle internal battles; feeling not good enough, not loved, or not seen. Pain, when left unresolved, can destroy potential. But what if pain could be the very place where power is born?

Pain does not have to be the end of your story. It can be the beginning of a new chapter. The Bible shows us many stories of young people who were broken, betrayed, or beaten down, but who rose above their pain and became powerful tools in God's hands.

Take the story of Joseph in Genesis. As a teenager, he was hated by his brothers, thrown into a pit, sold into slavery, falsely accused, and forgotten in prison. Every stage of his life was filled with pain and unfair treatment. But through it all, God was preparing him. Joseph didn't allow bitterness to define him. He kept his heart right and held on to his dreams. In the end, he rose to power in Egypt and became the very person who saved his family and nation during a crisis.

Pain Is Not the End

Teenagers must be taught that pain is real, but it is not final. Pain is not a sign of weakness; it is a part of life. What matters is what you do with it. Some allow pain to make them bitter, others allow it to make them better. The same fire that melts wax also hardens clay. You can decide whether the fire of your pain will melt your hope or harden your resolve.

God never wastes pain. Every tear you've cried can water the seeds of greatness in your future. The anger, the betrayal, the loneliness, God sees it all.

When you surrender your pain to God, He turns it into purpose. Your scars become your testimony. What hurt you can become what helps others.

Healing Comes Through Processing

Many teenagers today bottle up their emotions. They mask their pain behind social media filters, humor, rebellion, or isolation. But healing doesn't come from hiding. Healing comes from processing.

Talk to someone. Open up to a youth leader, a trusted friend, or a counselor. Pour your heart out to God in prayer. Jesus Christ understands your pain; He was betrayed, rejected, mocked, and crucified. He knows what it feels like to be alone, misunderstood, and hurt. Isaiah 53:3 says He was *"a man of sorrows, acquainted with grief."*

When you come to Him with your wounds, He doesn't push you away. He draws near. He begins a process of healing and restoration.

Your Pain Can Empower Others

One of the most powerful ways to turn pain into power is by helping others who are going through what you went through. If you've experienced rejection, you can be the one who welcomes others. If you've battled depression, you can be the voice that encourages someone to keep going. If you've been through abuse, your story can bring healing and hope to someone else.

2 Corinthians 1:4 says, *"He comforts us in all our troubles so that we can comfort others."* God wants to use your experience not only to heal you but to empower you to be a healer.

Many teenagers who've faced hardship have gone on to become leaders, artists, counselors, and advocates. The pain gave them insight, depth, and compassion. What once seemed like a weakness became their greatest strength.

The Role of the Church and Community

Churches, schools, and communities have a major role to play. We must create spaces where teenagers feel safe to talk about their pain without judgment. We must teach them not only to survive but to thrive. We must guide them to the truth that their worth is not defined by their wounds but by the One who heals them.

Youth ministries should encourage resilience. Testimonies should be shared often. Programs should be designed not just to entertain but to empower, teaching life skills, spiritual maturity, and emotional intelligence. Mentorship should be intentional.

A Final Word to the Teenager Reading This

You are not your pain. You are not your mistake. You are chosen, seen, loved, and called. What happened to you cannot change your purpose.

You have power inside of you. The same God who raised Jesus from the dead lives in you if you believe in Him. And that means no pain is too deep, no past too broken, and no mistake too great for Him to redeem.

Let your pain push you into prayer. Let it lead you to purpose. Let it drive you to compassion. And above all, let God turn your ashes into beauty, your crying into dancing, and your pain into power.

PART 4

HOW THE CHURCH CAN HELP

Chapter 16

Practical Ways the Church can Minister to Teens

16.1 Youth Programs

One of the most effective ways the Church can minister to teenagers today is by developing strong, engaging, and spiritually impactful youth programs. Today's teenagers are facing an increasingly complex world, characterized by rapid technology, shifting moral values, and heightened social pressures. As such, the Church must offer youth programs that are not only spiritually enriching but also culturally relevant and emotionally supportive.

Youth programs should go beyond simply gathering young people in a room. They must be purpose-driven, intentionally designed to meet the spiritual, emotional, intellectual, and social needs of teens. Teenagers are looking for belonging, guidance, and real answers to life's pressing questions. The Church must rise to the occasion with programs that connect them to God, community, and their purpose.

1. Faith-Centered Youth Fellowships

At the heart of every youth program should be a vibrant faith experience. Weekly or monthly youth fellowships provide teens with a safe space to learn the Word of God, ask questions, and experience the love of Christ in a setting tailored to their age group. These meetings should be interactive, allowing teens to share their challenges and testimonies while receiving sound biblical teaching.

This is also a powerful platform to train young people to develop spiritual disciplines such as prayer, fasting, and studying Scripture. When teens see that Christianity is not just a religion, but a relationship with Jesus Christ, their hearts begin to open. Leaders must also be approachable and trained to deal with youth-related issues sensitively, including topics like puberty, peer pressure, and mental health.

2. Creative Arts and Talent-Based Ministries

Youth programs that include creative arts such as music, dance, drama, poetry, spoken word, and media production attract teens who may otherwise feel disengaged. These platforms allow them to express their faith in ways that are natural and exciting for them.

When teenagers see that their talents can be used to glorify God and edify others, they are more likely to commit to the Church and grow spiritually.

Involving youth in church activities such as leading worship, acting in biblical skits, or designing media content for services helps them take ownership of their faith. These outlets also serve as discipleship tools. As they rehearse, create, and perform, leaders can use those moments to teach biblical values and develop leadership skills.

3. Leadership and Discipleship Training

Every youth program should be intentional about raising young leaders. Discipleship is not just for adults; teens too must be discipled to become the next generation of Godly leaders. This can be done through one-on-one mentoring, small discipleship groups, and leadership training classes. Teens should be challenged to take responsibility, serve others, and live according to God's Word.

Assigning teens roles within the youth ministry, such as planning events, leading Bible studies, or heading service projects, instills confidence and nurtures spiritual maturity. When young people are trained early in leadership, they grow up with a sense of spiritual purpose and responsibility.

4. Community Outreach and Mission Projects

Another important aspect of youth programs is service. Teens need to understand that faith without works is dead. Organizing local outreach projects, such as visiting orphanages, cleaning community areas, or distributing food to the needy, can help teens see the gospel in action. Mission trips, whether local or international, also open their eyes to the needs of the world and how they can make a difference.

Such activities build compassion, teamwork, and resilience in teenagers. They learn to appreciate what they have and become less self-centered as they serve others. It is also an excellent way to expose them to different cultures, conditions, and the global body of Christ.

5. Life Skills and Career Guidance

Youth programs should also include practical sessions that address the realities of teenage life. Seminars on career planning, university admissions, entrepreneurship, financial literacy, and dealing with peer pressure are vital.

The Church can invite professionals from different fields to speak, mentor, and guide teens in discovering and developing their potential.

By offering real-life tools and advice, the Church shows that it cares about every area of a young person's life, not just their spiritual growth. This holistic approach helps teens see the Church as a relevant and valuable place for guidance and support.

6. Retreats, Camps, and Conferences

Periodic retreats, youth camps, and conferences are powerful tools for spiritual awakening and bonding. When teens step away from their routine and enter an atmosphere focused on God, surrounded by like-minded peers, their hearts become more open to divine encounters. Many testimonies of salvation, healing, and calling have emerged from such events.

These settings allow for intense teaching, worship, fellowship, and fun, all of which contribute to spiritual and emotional growth. Camps also help youth leaders identify potential in teens and give them more focused mentoring.

In conclusion, youth programs are not just a "nice extra" but a critical ministry in the life of any church. A thriving youth ministry can determine the future of the church. When teenagers are ministered to effectively, they grow into adults who love and serve God wholeheartedly. It's time for the Church to invest prayerfully, creatively, and strategically in youth programs that will raise a generation rooted in Christ and ready to transform the world.

16.2 Mentorship

Mentorship is one of the most effective and life-transforming ways the Church can minister to teenagers today. In a world where young people are constantly bombarded by mixed messages from media, peers, and social platforms, the presence of a Godly mentor provides stability, clarity, and a model to follow. Mentorship allows teens to see how faith is lived out in real life and to walk closely with someone who genuinely cares for their spiritual, emotional, and personal development.

Why Mentorship Matters

Teenagers are in a critical stage of development, they are forming their identity, values, and vision for life. At this stage, they often wrestle with questions like: Who am I? What is my purpose? Does God care about my future? Mentors step into this space not with all the answers, but with a heart willing to listen, pray, guide, and journey alongside a young person.

Proverbs 27:17 says, "As iron sharpens iron, so a man sharpens the countenance of his friend." Mentorship is a sharpening process. When teens spend time with mentors, people who love God, walk in wisdom, and are willing to invest time, they grow stronger in character, more rooted in the Word, and better equipped to handle life's pressures.

Who Can Be a Mentor?

A mature believer with a passion for youth, a consistent walk with God, and a willingness to be available can be an effective mentor. Young adults, professionals, retired persons, married couples, pastors and ministers can serve as mentors to teens. What matters most is consistency, authenticity, and a heart that reflects Christ.

Titus 2:3–5 teaches that older believers should teach and guide the younger ones. This biblical model of mentorship should be embraced by every local church.

Building a Mentorship Culture in the Church

For mentorship to thrive, the Church must create a safe and structured environment. Here are some practical ways to do this:

- *Identify willing mentors:* Invite spiritually mature members of the congregation who have a heart for youth to serve as mentors. Provide basic training on how to mentor with wisdom, grace, and biblical principles.

- *Match mentors and mentees prayerfully:* Consider personality, background, gender, and interests when pairing mentors with teens. Encourage mentors to meet with their mentees at least twice a month, whether in person, online, or over a phone call.

- *Set clear expectations:* Mentorship is not about fixing teens or controlling their decisions, but about walking with them, helping them discover God's purpose, and being present.

- *Create accountability and oversight:* Assign a youth leader or pastoral staff member to oversee the mentorship program. This ensures quality, provides guidance to mentors, and addresses any issues that may arise.

- *Encourage relational discipleship:* Encourage mentors to include teens in their daily lives; invite them to family dinners, involve them in community service, go on prayer walks, or do Bible study together. Teens learn more from what they see than from what they hear.

Testimonies of Impact

In churches where mentorship is practiced, the impact is undeniable. Teens report feeling more confident, understood, and connected to the Church. Many grow deeper in their faith and even step into leadership roles earlier because of the guidance and encouragement from their mentors.

One 16-year-old girl shared, "My mentor is like a big sister to me. She listens when I feel overwhelmed and prays with me. She helps me believe that God has a good plan for my life." Another teenage boy said, "Before, I used to skip church and didn't care But when my mentor started meeting with me and teaching me how to read the Bible, everything changed."

Challenges and Wisdom

Mentorship is not always easy. Teens may be inconsistent, distracted, or unresponsive at times. Mentors need patience and prayer. It's also essential to maintain boundaries, especially in one-on-one relationships between opposite genders; mentors should never counsel in isolation without accountability.

Finally, mentorship must be Spirit-led. Each teen is unique, and only the Holy Spirit can give mentors the wisdom and insight to meet their specific needs. Churches should regularly pray for mentors and mentees and celebrate the wins, no matter how small.

Mentorship is not just a strategy; it is a calling. Jesus Christ mentored twelve disciples and transformed the world through them. The Church today must rise and take mentorship seriously. It is a powerful tool to raise strong, Godly teens who will become the next generation of leaders, pastors, missionaries, and righteous influencers. Let every church hear the call and prepare the mentors who will shape the future.

16.3 Safe Spaces

A safe space is not simply a physical location, but a culture; a spiritual atmosphere of trust, openness, and grace. It is a place where teens can remove their masks, speak their minds, and open their hearts, knowing that they will not be ignored. In a world where social media often promotes perfectionism and comparison, the Church must stand out as a refuge of authenticity and unconditional love.

What Does a Safe Space Look Like?

A safe space within the Church could be a youth hall, a fellowship room, a prayer corner, or even an outdoor gathering area. However, beyond the physical setting, it is defined by the kind of people present: leaders and volunteers who are trained, compassionate, and committed to building trust with teenagers. These leaders listen more than they speak, ask questions without judgment, and model Christ-like empathy.

Safe spaces must be built on four pillars:

- *Confidentiality:* Teens must know that what they share in a group or one-on-one setting will not be used against them or spread around. Boundaries must be clearly communicated and respected.

- *Non-judgmental Presence:* The Church must avoid quick correction or condemnation. Teens often deal with doubts, struggles, and sin. A safe space allows them to bring their real selves before God and trusted leaders, even before they are fully ready to change.

- *Inclusion:* Every teen, regardless of background, race, appearance, or struggles, should feel welcome. Jesus Christ was a friend of those society pushed away. The Church must reflect His heart.

- *Encouragement Toward Growth:* A safe space does not mean spiritual passivity. It is a place where grace and truth meet. Teens are gently led to grow in maturity, identity, and purpose in Christ.

Practical Examples of Safe Spaces in Action

- *Weekly Teen Gatherings:* Create weekly youth meetings that go beyond Bible study and include open forums for honest discussion. Let teens talk about mental health, sexuality, and peer pressure, in the light of Scripture, without fear.

- *Mentorship Circles:* Organize small mentorship groups where one adult leads a group of 3–5 teens. This allows closer relationships to form and helps teens find trusted adults to confide in.

- *Creative Expression Zones:* Some teens find it easier to open up through art, music, or writing. Provide them with opportunities to express themselves creatively in a judgment-free zone. You may be surprised at the depth of spiritual truth they release through these mediums.

- *Prayer & Counseling Rooms:* Have a designated area in the Church where teens can come for prayer, quiet reflection, or to talk to a spiritual counselor. The availability of trained counselors or peer support teams can make a world of difference.

- *Online Safe Spaces:* In this digital generation, the Church can also create moderated WhatsApp groups, Discord servers, or other platforms where teens can connect and ask questions about faith and life in a safe online community.

The Role of the Holy Spirit

Ultimately, safe spaces are not just made by physical setups or good leadership; they are created by the presence of the Holy Spirit. He is the Spirit of comfort, truth, and freedom. As we welcome His presence into our youth spaces, we can expect healing to flow, identity to be restored, and boldness to arise in the lives of teenagers.

God desires that the Church be a refuge, a city of hope for the young. When we provide safe spaces, we not only help teens survive their challenges, but we empower them to thrive and become mighty warriors for Christ.

16.4 Financial Empowerment

One of the most overlooked but deeply necessary areas in ministering to teenagers is *financial empowerment*. While many churches emphasize spiritual growth, emotional healing, and character development, it is equally important to teach teens how to handle money wisely and prepare for financial independence. Teenagers today are bombarded with materialism, social media pressure, and consumerism from a young age, yet they are rarely taught how to steward finances with Godly wisdom.

The Church can play a vital role in filling this gap, not only to prevent future financial hardship but to raise a generation of financially responsible and Kingdom-minded young people.

1. Teach Biblical Principles of Stewardship

The foundation of financial empowerment must be rooted in Scripture. Teens need to know that money is not evil, but the love of money is what leads to evil (1 Timothy 6:10). They should be taught that **everything belongs to God** (Psalm 24:1) and that we are merely stewards of what He entrusts to us.

Churches can organize youth Bible studies or workshops on topics such as:

- Tithing and giving generously (Malachi 3:10; 2 Corinthians 9:7)

- Avoiding debt (Proverbs 22:7)

- Saving and investing (Proverbs 21:20)

- Contentment and gratitude (Philippians 4:11–13)

By learning these principles early, teens develop a healthy and Godly mindset toward finances.

2. Offer Practical Financial Literacy Training

Beyond spiritual teaching, the Church can organize *practical financial literacy classes* that include topics such as budgeting, saving, managing a bank account, using money apps, understanding credit, and setting financial goals. These skills are often not taught in schools, but they are crucial for future success.

Financial experts or responsible Christian adults within the church can volunteer to run *quarterly seminars or mentoring sessions*. Churches can also partner with local organizations or financial institutions that offer youth-targeted programs.

Hands-on activities like budgeting challenges, mock business setups, or "financial boot camps" can make learning both fun and engaging.

3. Encourage Entrepreneurship and Talent Development

Many teenagers have unique gifts, creativity, and ideas that, if nurtured, can become sources of income. The Church can support these young talents by:

- Organizing *entrepreneurship days* where teens showcase and sell products or services.

- Helping them start small businesses such as digital design, tutoring, baking, writing, or music lessons.

- Providing *mentorship from business-minded adults* who can guide them in how to build, grow, and manage their own enterprises.

Through entrepreneurship, teens learn responsibility, discipline, and the importance of work—all of which are Biblical values (Proverbs 10:4, Colossians 3:23).

4. Create a Teen Job Board or Volunteer Exchange

Churches can create opportunities for teens to earn small incomes or gain work experience within the church or community. For example:

- Babysitting during church events

- Helping with technical equipment, video editing, or media management

- Running errands for elderly members

- Organizing or decorating for youth events

These activities teach responsibility, time management, and the value of honest labor. Even small stipends or tokens of appreciation can go a long way in building confidence and financial responsibility.

5. Model a Culture of Generosity and Responsibility

Finally, financial empowerment is not just about making or managing money; it is also about developing the heart. The Church must model and teach that financial blessings are tools for serving others, supporting missions, and advancing the Kingdom of God.

When teens see a culture where generosity, planning, and accountability are normal, they are more likely to follow suit. The Church should challenge teens to set aside part of their money, no matter how little, for giving to others in need, whether it's sponsoring a child, supporting missionaries, or helping a classmate in need.

By equipping teenagers with financial wisdom, the Church is not only helping them avoid future pitfalls but also raising up stewards who can fund the vision of God. Financial empowerment is discipleship in action; it enables teens to walk in freedom, responsibility, and purpose, both now and in the years to come.

16.5 Spiritual Training and Prayer

In the midst of today's rapidly changing world, teenagers are being exposed to an array of ideologies, temptations, and spiritual confusion. While the world is busy discipling our youth through media, peer pressure, and cultural trends, the Church must rise to the occasion and intentionally invest in spiritual training and prayer for the next generation. This is not optional; it is vital. The future of the Church and the spiritual destiny of our youth depend on it.

1. Teaching Teens to Know God Personally

Spiritual training begins with helping teens establish a personal relationship with God through Jesus Christ. This is more than attending Church services; it's about nurturing a real, living connection with the Lord. The Church should ensure that teens understand the foundational truths of salvation, grace, the cross, and the new life in Christ. Youth Bible classes, small discipleship groups, and one-on-one mentorship can help them grow in knowledge and spiritual maturity.

Regular teachings on the love of God, the work of the Holy Spirit, and the authority of the Bible can help teenagers develop a solid spiritual foundation. Teens should be encouraged to ask questions, seek answers, and wrestle with their faith in a safe and guided environment.

2. Training in the Word and Discipleship

Teenagers need systematic teaching of the Bible, not just motivational talks. They should be trained in how to read, interpret, and apply Scripture in their daily lives. Providing them with Bible study tools, reading plans, and the opportunity to lead devotions or youth Bible discussions will empower them spiritually.

The Church should also implement mentorship programs where spiritually mature believers walk alongside teens, guiding them through life's challenges while modeling Christian character. These relationships help teens see how faith works practically and build a strong community of accountability.

3. Creating a Culture of Prayer Among Teenagers

Prayer is not a religious duty; it is the lifeline of every believer. Yet many teenagers see prayer as boring, mechanical, or intimidating. The Church must demystify prayer for young people and teach them its power, purpose, and joy.

Practical steps include organizing youth prayer meetings, early morning or evening prayer chains, and times of fasting and intercession tailored to young people. Teach them to pray for their schools, families, friends, and nations. Encourage them to pray with boldness and expectation.

Create an atmosphere where teenagers feel comfortable expressing themselves in prayer, whether it's through spoken words, writing, music, or silent meditation. Some teens may not know how to start praying; equip them with scriptural prayer guides (like the Lord's Prayer, the Psalms) and offer teachings on how to hear God's voice.

4. Involving Teens in Corporate Church Prayer

Teenagers should not be excluded from the Church's main prayer life. Involve them in Sunday intercessory groups, all-night vigils, or prayer altar sessions. Assign roles such as praying for specific topics, leading short exhortations, or reading prayer scriptures, to help them feel responsible and included.

When teens are allowed to participate, they grow in confidence and begin to see prayer as something they *do*, not just something *adults do for them*. It becomes their personal weapon and spiritual strength.

5. Helping Teens Experience the Power of the Holy Spirit

Spiritual training is incomplete without introducing teenagers to the power of the Holy Spirit. Many young people battle depression, confusion, and peer pressure. They need the empowerment that only the Holy Spirit gives: wisdom, boldness, discernment, and joy.

Teach on the baptism of the Holy Spirit and spiritual gifts, allowing time for teens to seek and experience these things in a respectful and scripturally sound manner. Create space for them to pray for one another, give testimonies, and use their spiritual gifts in youth services.

When teens experience the presence and power of God for themselves, their faith becomes real and unshakable. They are no longer just attendees; they become warriors, intercessors, and leaders in their generation.

Spiritual training and prayer are not just Church programs; they are the tools for building strong, Godly teens who will stand firm in a dark world. Every Church must prioritize this with urgency and vision. Our youth don't just need activities; they need an encounter with the living God. And it is the Church's divine responsibility to lead them there.

Chapter 17

Raising a Generation of Purpose-Driven Teenagers

17.1 Equipping teens to discover their calling and make a Godly impact in society.

In today's rapidly changing world, teenagers are bombarded with endless distractions and conflicting messages about who they are and what their lives should look like. Social media platforms shape their identity, peer pressure influences their choices, and society often misguides them about success and purpose. Amid all this, the Church and Christian homes are called to raise a generation of purpose-driven teenagers; young men and women who understand that they were created by God for a reason and are empowered to live out that calling.

1. Understanding Purpose from a Biblical View

Purpose is not just about career, status, or worldly success; it is about fulfilling God's original intent for one's life. Teenagers must learn that God has a unique plan for each of them. Jeremiah 1:5 says, *"Before I formed you in the womb I knew you; before you were born I sanctified you; I ordained you a prophet to the nations."* This scripture reminds us that divine purpose precedes birth. Teaching teens that their lives matter to God helps them resist the lie that they are insignificant.

Helping teenagers discover purpose begins with helping them **know God personally**. The closer they walk with Jesus, the more they can discern His plans. Purpose is not something we invent; it is something we discover through prayer, studying God's Word, and walking in obedience.

2. Creating Environments for Discovery

Churches and youth ministries must intentionally create environments where purpose can be discovered. Sunday services alone are not enough. Teenagers need mentorship, platforms to serve, and consistent exposure to Godly models.

Encourage:

- *Purpose Discovery Classes*: Small group sessions where teenagers learn about spiritual gifts, biblical purpose, and personal growth.

- *Ministry Exposure*: Let teens try different areas of service (music, drama, outreach, teaching children, etc.) to see where they feel most alive and fruitful.

- *One-on-One Mentorship*: God often uses people to help confirm and guide a calling. Assign older youth or adult mentors to walk with teens through life's questions.

In these environments, teens begin to see their strengths and natural inclinations as potential clues to what God might be calling them to do.

3. Equipping Teens with Biblical Identity

One major obstacle to walking in purpose is confusion about identity. A purpose-driven life begins with understanding who you are in Christ. Many teens struggle with insecurity, rejection, body image, or feeling unworthy. When teens know they are **sons and daughters of God,** loved, accepted, and called, they can face the world with courage.

Ephesians 2:10 says, *"For we are His workmanship, created in Christ Jesus for good works, which God prepared beforehand that we should walk in them."* This verse teaches teens that their identity and purpose are rooted in Christ, not in trends, likes, or popularity.

Churches and parents must speak life over their teens. Declare over them who they are in Christ. Teach them confessions of identity: "I am chosen, I am gifted, I am called, I am blessed."

4. Training in Godly Character and Discipline

A purpose-driven teenager is not only gifted but also mature in character. Gifts can open doors, but it is a Godly character that sustains a life of impact. Teach teens the importance of:

- *Integrity:* Doing what is right even when no one is watching.

- *Discipline:* Managing time, emotions, and energy to pursue goals.

- *Responsibility:* Being faithful in small things prepares you for greater things.

- *Servanthood:* Greatness in God's Kingdom comes from serving others.

- Give teenagers responsibility in the Church.

Let them help in organizing events, leading younger kids, or running youth fellowships. These opportunities train their character and build leadership skills.

5. Encouraging Academic and Practical Excellence

Being purpose-driven includes excelling in academics and practical skills. Daniel and his friends in Babylon were ten times better than others because they were well-taught, wise, and full of God's Spirit (Daniel 1:17-20). Encourage teenagers to see school as a mission field and a platform to prepare for future influence.

Support teens in developing their talents: writing, coding, public speaking, cooking, sports, music, etc., and teach them that every skill, when surrendered to God, can be used for His glory.

A teenager who becomes a doctor, teacher, engineer, or entrepreneur can fulfill God's calling just as much as a pastor or missionary, if they remain obedient to Christ.

6. Helping Teens See Their World as Their Mission Field

A purpose-driven teen lives to *make a Godly impact* in society. The Gospel is not just for the Church; it must overflow into schools, communities, and nations. Train teenagers to be salt and light wherever they go.

Empower them to:

- Stand up for truth and righteousness.

- Love people unconditionally, especially those who are hurting.

- Use their voice to speak hope and justice.

- Share the Gospel boldly, yet wisely.

Encourage them to start school Bible clubs, social media outreach, community clean-up days, or music nights where God is glorified.

Teenagers are bold by nature; when that boldness is harnessed for God, great things happen.

7. Creating a Culture of Prayer and Sensitivity to God's Voice

The foundation of a purpose-driven life is communion with God. Prayer is not a ritual; it is a relationship. Teach teenagers to pray, fast, listen to God, and write down what He tells them. Encourage them to:

- Have a daily devotion time.

- Journal their prayers and dreams.

- Seek guidance before making decisions.

- Obey the small promptings of the Holy Spirit.

When teens become sensitive to God's voice early in life, they avoid many mistakes and grow in wisdom.

8. The Role of Parents, Pastors, and Teachers

The journey of raising purpose-driven teens is a partnership. Parents, pastors, and teachers must walk together in love, correction, encouragement, and example. Parents must affirm their teens consistently and involve them in family spiritual life. Pastors must not underestimate teenagers but give them real responsibilities. Teachers in schools must be reminded that they are shaping destinies, not just teaching lessons.

As a Church, let us stop underestimating our youth. Let us call out their potential, guide them patiently, and challenge them to aim higher. With the right support, teenagers can be world changers in their generation.

Raising a generation of purpose-driven teenagers is not optional; it is urgent. The future of the Church, society, and nations depends on what we deposit in them today. Let us equip them to know God, discover His purpose for their lives, and make a lasting impact wherever they go. The time is now to empower our teenagers to rise and shine, for their light has come, and the Glory of the Lord is rising upon them (Isaiah 60:1).

Chapter 18

A Call to Parents, Leaders, and the Church

18.1 Uniting the Body of Christ to Rescue, Rebuild, and Release This Generation into Their Destiny

The teenagers of today stand at a critical crossroads. They face unprecedented challenges, from digital addiction, peer pressure, violence, and broken homes to spiritual dryness. At the same time, they carry immense potential. They are creative, bold, innovative, and full of dreams. But they need guidance. It is therefore urgent for the Body of Christ, parents, leaders, and churches, to unite and respond to God's call to rescue, rebuild, and release this generation.

1. Rescuing a Generation at Risk

Many teenagers today are spiritually drowning. Their minds are under attack by secular ideologies, media influence, and moral relativism. Some are victims of abuse, neglect, poverty, or gang pressure. Others suffer in silence from depression, rejection, or suicidal thoughts. We cannot afford to sit back and watch.

Rescue starts with intercession. Before we act, we must first stand in the gap through prayer. Just as Moses stood between God and Israel, and Esther stood for her people, we must stand for our youth. Prayer breaks spiritual chains and opens the way for divine intervention. Every local church must raise a generation of intercessors who will cry out to God on behalf of the youth.

Rescue also means availability. Parents and leaders must make time for teenagers. Many youth are not rebellious by nature; they are simply reacting to neglect or misunderstanding. They need listeners more than lecturers. A parent who kneels to pray with their child will often have a child who stands tall in faith.

The Good Shepherd left the ninety-nine to go after the one lost sheep. In the same spirit, we must go out of our way to reach the teens who have fallen into bad company, those who no longer come to church, and those who've lost hope in life. We must go to them with compassion, not condemnation.

2. Rebuilding What Has Been Broken

Teenagers often come from broken homes, carry broken dreams, and live in broken systems. God is calling His people to be *repairers of the breach* (Isaiah 58:12). Once rescued, these youth need to be rebuilt emotionally, mentally, spiritually, and socially.

The home is the first altar. Parents, especially fathers, must reclaim their role as spiritual leaders. A father's affirmation builds confidence, while a mother's prayers birth destiny. Homes should be safe places where truth is taught, worship is modeled, and love flows freely. If we want strong teens, we must rebuild strong homes.

Churches must become training grounds, not just gathering grounds. We must move beyond entertaining youth to equipping them. Discipleship, mentoring, and service opportunities should be available for every teenager. Let them serve in media, ushering, music, missions, and teaching. Involvement builds ownership and strengthens identity in Christ.

Leaders must lead by example. Whether in church, schools, or the community, teens are watching. They imitate what we tolerate. Let us show them how to love God, treat others, make wise decisions, and stand firm in adversity. Hypocrisy turns them away; authenticity draws them close.

3. Releasing Them into Their God-Given Destiny

God has not called our teenagers to just survive; He has called them to thrive and influence nations. They carry gifts, anointing, and callings that must be stirred and released. We must stop underestimating their capacity and start empowering them to walk in purpose.

Release begins with recognition. Just as Paul the apostle saw potential in Timothy, we must identify the talents, passions, and callings in our youth. Every teenager has something unique to offer. Some are called to preach, others to lead in business, media, sports, music, or politics. Our job is to nurture what God has deposited in them.

Then, we must empower them. This generation does not need control; they need guidance. Give them the Word. Show them how to use their spiritual gifts. Trust them with responsibility. Let them lead youth services, initiate outreach programs, and share their testimonies. Support them with resources, counsel, and spiritual covering.

Finally, we must launch them with a blessing. When Jesus Christ was baptized, He heard His Father say, "This is My beloved Son in whom I am well pleased." That affirmation propelled Jesus into ministry. Likewise, when we speak life over our teens, it gives them the confidence to step into their calling. The church must be a launching pad, not a holding pen.

4. Uniting the Body of Christ: A Collective Responsibility

This work cannot rest on one person or group alone. Rescuing, re-building, and releasing teenagers requires unity in the Body of Christ. Denominations, ministries, and families must come together with one voice and one heart. Our differences should not divide us when the mission is this urgent.

Joint youth conferences, united prayer vigils, and city-wide outreach initiatives can go a long way. Let churches pool their resources to start youth centers, after-school programs, and skills development work-shops. Let parents form prayer groups to intercede for their children and communities. Let pastors prioritize the youth as part of their vision.

Jesus said, *"A kingdom divided against itself cannot stand"* (Mark 3:24). The devil loves disunity, but God blesses unity with power. When we come together across cultural, ethnic, and generational lines, heaven backs us up. Together, we can take back this generation from the hands of the enemy.

5. The Urgency of Now

Time is short. The enemy is not waiting. He is actively sowing lies, rebel-lion, and confusion into the hearts of our teenagers. But the Holy Spirit is also moving, calling the Church to arise with compassion, strategy, and fire.

Let us no longer say, "Someone else will do it."

You are the parent, leader, teacher, pastor, or intercessor God wants to use.

You are the light in their darkness.

You are the voice they are waiting to hear. *You* are the one who will lead them to Jesus.

It starts in our homes, our churches, our classrooms, and our streets. If we unite as the Body of Christ, loving, teaching, praying, and empowering, then we will see teenagers not only saved but also filled with the Spirit, rooted in truth, and released into destiny.

God has not given up on this generation, and neither should we. Teenagers today are not a lost cause; they are *God's harvest field and His army in training*. Let us arise, unite, and act to rescue the hurting, rebuild the broken, and release the called.

Heaven is watching. Hell is trembling. The time is now.

HOPE FOR THE NEXT GENERATION

As we draw this book to a close, it is vital to end not with fear or despair over the state of today's teenagers, but with a firm declaration of **hope**

Hope grounded in God, in the potential of our youth, and in the power of love, mentorship, and intentional discipleship. The world may seem increasingly complicated for teenagers, but we believe that with the right support systems, spiritual guidance, and practical tools, this generation can rise up and lead with wisdom, righteousness, and courage.

First and foremost, we must remember that God is never taken by surprise. Every generation is born within the timeline of His divine plan. The teenagers of today were born for *such a time as this*. Despite the rise in moral confusion, identity crises, social pressure, and digital distractions, the Lord still has a purpose for this generation. The same God who used young David to defeat Goliath, young Mary to carry the Messiah, and young Timothy to lead in ministry is still raising up young people today who will carry His fire and change their communities and nations.

God's plans are redemptive. He is The God who brings beauty from ashes and hope from hopelessness. Teenagers struggling with rejection, addictions, fatherlessness, or low self-esteem are not forgotten by God. In fact, they are at the center of His heart. As parents, pastors, mentors, and leaders, our role is to believe in them, speak life into them, and walk beside them through their journey of discovery and healing.

We Must Keep Planting Seeds

The teenage years are not just turbulent, they are also fertile. Teenagers are searching for meaning, acceptance, and identity. This is the perfect soil for planting seeds of truth, love, faith, and purpose. While it may seem that some seeds take longer to sprout, we must remember the words of Scripture: *"Let us not grow weary while doing good, for in due season we shall reap if we do not lose heart"* (Galatians 6:9).

Every youth program, every encouraging word, every prayer, and every act of kindness is a seed. Even when we do not see immediate results, we must trust the process. The harvest is coming.

The Church Has a Critical Role to Play

One of the most powerful tools God has placed on earth to impact the next generation is *the Church*. However, we must ask ourselves: Are our churches truly accessible and relevant to teenagers today? Are we equipping them to face real-world challenges, or are we just entertaining them once a week?

The Church must become a safe space where teenagers are heard, valued, and discipled.

Youth groups should be more than games and music; they should be schools of purpose and launchpads of destiny. Teenagers need opportunities to lead, serve, and explore their spiritual gifts. We must also intentionally build intergenerational bridges, where older believers mentor and walk with the younger ones, offering wisdom, counsel, and a living example of faith.

The Church should also partner with families, schools, and communities to create wraparound support systems that empower teenagers.

This means providing mentorship, tutoring, career guidance, financial literacy, mental health awareness, and above all, spiritual covering.

Teenagers Are Not Just the Future; They Are the Present

Too often, we refer to young people as "the leaders of tomorrow." While well-intentioned, this statement delays their impact. Many teenagers are ready to lead today, if only given the platform and support.

The world is already using teenagers to set trends, influence millions on social media, and drive innovation. The Church must likewise create avenues for young people to influence culture with righteousness and truth.

We must believe that a 16-year-old can preach the Gospel boldly. A 16-year-old can organize a citywide prayer meeting. A 17-year-old can mentor younger kids. A 15-year-old can write books, compose songs, or start a Christian YouTube channel. Let's stop waiting for them to grow up before we empower them. Let's empower them now.

There Is Hope in Prayer and Intercession

Finally, our greatest weapon in this battle for the soul of the next generation is *prayer*. Prayer can go where we cannot. It can reach the heart of a rebellious teen in ways that no sermon can. Through prayer, strongholds are broken, destinies are unlocked, and lives are transformed. Every revival throughout history had one thing in common: young people on fire for God, and people praying behind the scenes.

Let us pray for teenagers with fervency and faith, that they would encounter God personally, that they would be set free from the lies of the enemy, that they would be filled with the Holy Spirit, and walk in power. Let us also pray for parents, teachers, and mentors to be filled with wisdom, grace, and patience.

There is also great power in teaching teenagers how to pray for themselves. A praying teen is a weapon against the enemy. We must teach them that prayer is not just a duty, but a lifeline, a relationship, a lifestyle. When teenagers begin to intercede for their friends, schools, and families, revival will come.

WORDS OF ENCOURAGEMENT

We conclude this book with confidence that the future is bright, because Jesus is still on the throne, and the next generation is blessed. We believe that out of this generation will rise Daniels, Esthers, Joshuas, and Deborahs. They will carry the gospel into every sphere of society: education, media, business, technology, and the arts.

To every parent, teacher, pastor, or mentor reading this book: Do not give up. Your labor is not in vain. Your voice matters. Your prayers matter. Your presence matters. The seeds you are sowing will bear eternal impact.

And to every teenager reading this book: You are loved. You are chosen. You were born for greatness. Don't let the noise of the world drown out the Voice of your Creator. Seek Him. Follow Him. Trust Him.

Together, let us raise a generation that knows God, walks in truth, and lives with purpose.

INVITATION

Our righteousness is of the Lord. It is therefore necessary for us to be part of the Body of Christ and to have a personal relationship with the Lord to become children of God.

John 1:12-13 *"But as many as received Him, to them gave He power to become the sons of God, even to them that believe on His name: Which were born, not of blood, nor of the will of the flesh, nor of the will of man, but of God."* Do you want to be confident in your spiritual battles in prayer? Do you want to give your heart and your life to God so He can dwell in you forever? You can pray the following prayer to the Lord.

Heavenly Father, I come to You through Your only begotten Son Jesus Christ. I am very sorry for my sins, I repent of my sins and iniquities. Please forgive me, cleanse me from all my unrighteousness through the Blood of Your Son Jesus Christ. I want You to come into my heart and save me. Lord Jesus, I believe you died on the cross for my sins and was raised again for my justification. I receive You as the Lord and Master of my life. I ask You to lead and guide me every day in Your Word, and I ask for the power to obey You. I choose to obey You and follow Your will for my life. Thank You Lord, for coming into my heart. Thank You Holy Spirit for writing my name in the Lamb's book of Life. In Jesus' Name I pray. Amen.

If you are a Christian already, and you want to enter into the victorious life of Christ, to be set free from the powers of darkness and from the dominion of sin. If you want to renew your commitment and covenant with the Lord, you can likewise pray the above prayer.

If you need to agree in prayer with a minister to help you more in your prayer life and in your spiritual battles, write or call us, and we shall be delighted to assist you more in the Name of our Lord Jesus Christ.

To contact the author, please write to:

Miradorplein 39, 6222 TE Maastricht
The Netherlands

Or call: +31 (0) 685 261 335
E-mail: info@shekinahevangelicalchurch.com

Please feel free to share your testimony about how this book has helped you. You are also welcome to include your prayer requests.

ABOUT THE AUTHOR

The author of this book, Pastor Mariana Vanstipelen, is a passionate mentor, Bible teacher, and advocate for youth empowerment. With years of experience working with teenagers in both faith-based and community settings, she brings a deep understanding of their struggles and potential, and offers practical and hopeful solutions to help them overcome and flourish.

A wife and mother of two children: Eunice and Joshua, Mariana's mission is to guide the next generation through Spiritual truth, practical Wisdom, and unconditional Love. '*Teenagers' World*' reflects her heart to see every young person thrive, dream big, and live with purpose.

To God be the glory!

OTHER BOOKS BY THE SAME AUTHOR

1. Biblical Principles of Long Life

2. Converting Mistakes to Miracles

3. The Creative Power of Prayer

4. Seven Ways God Answers Prayers

5. 70 Kinds of Prayers

6. Prayer For Healing

7. The Impact of Fasting in Prayer

8. Faith Versus Fear

9. Forgive

10. A Happy Christian

11. JESUS-CHRIST, The Bread of Life

12. JESUS-CHRIST, The Word of God

13. Power to Prosper

14. The Fruit of The Spirit

15. The Hem of His Garment

16. The HOLY SPIRIT

17. The King of kings

18. The Mantle of Power

19. The Rhema of God

20. The Shekinah of God

21. The Upper Room

22. Understanding The Church (Revelation)

23. The Heaven of A Good Marriage

24. 70 Keys for A Good Marriage

25. How to Choose a Godly Spouse

26. Maintaining the Marriage Covenant

27. The Marriage of Isaac and Rebekkah

28. Le Paradis d'un bon mariage (French)

BLESSINGS

As you close the pages of *The World of Teenagers Today*, may your heart be filled with hope, vision, and renewed purpose. May the truths, insights, and encouragement in these chapters plant lasting seeds of love and transformation.

To Every Teenager Reading This Book

May you know that you are not forgotten, not overlooked, and never too young to make a difference.

May the Lord reveal His purpose for your life in powerful and personal ways.

May you rise above confusion, peer pressure, and fear, and walk boldly in your God-given identity.

You are loved, chosen, and destined for greatness;

May wisdom guide your steps, and Godly friendships surround your journey.

You are the light of your generation.

To Every Parent and Guardian

May God give you patience, strength, and insight to nurture your teen with grace and truth.

May your home be a safe haven where love heals, wisdom flows, and Christ reigns.

May the Holy Spirit lead you with divine peace and courage.

You are not alone; He who gave you this assignment will also equip you.

May your prayers for your child be answered with joy and testimonies.

To Every Pastor and Youth Leader

May God refresh your calling to serve this generation with passion and power.

May God give you discernment to speak life, to model truth, and to mentor with integrity.

Your labor is not in vain; every seed sown in love will bear fruit in due season.

May God use you as a bridge between Heaven and the hearts of young people.

Continue to stand in the gap; your voice matters, your presence counts.

To Mentors, Teachers, and Community Builders

May you be filled with compassion, creativity, and clarity as you walk alongside teenagers.

May your influence be Godly, your words seasoned with grace, and your example a testimony of Christ.

Where there is brokenness, may you be a vessel of healing. Where there is searching, may you point to the One who is the Way, the Truth, and the Life.

You are a vital part of God's strategy for the next generation.

"The Lord bless you and keep you;
The Lord make His face shine upon you,
And be gracious to you;
The Lord lift up His countenance upon you,

And give you peace." (Numbers 6:24-26).

You are called to impact the world, one teen, one prayer, one word of hope at a time.

You are part of God's answer for this generation.

The future is bright because Jesus is with us, and teenagers are rising.

Let the world hear your voice. Let heaven hear your prayers.

The next generation is loved, led, and lit with purpose.

Amen.

NOTES